MY STORY GODS GLORY

The story of a walking miracle

Phillip O. Hanks

E-book ISBN: 979-8-9875742-2-5

Paperback ISBN: 979-8-9875742-3-2

First paperback edition January 2023

Book cover design by Phillip O. Hanks

Printed in the United States of America

Table of Contents

DEDICATION

To my brother, Terrence (Dinah) and my mother, Inez. I love you and miss you so much! To my wife, Tiva; my son Deon (Brittany); my daughter Alyssa; my son Cammeren; my son Collier; and my daughter Aliya. To my brother-in-law, Ron; To the Glovers, Simmons, Smiths, Williams, Banks, McCoy, Andrews, Givens and Robinson families, Thank you! To my sister, Idelle (Dennis) and my oldest brother, Gerald (Deborah), to my nieces; Nicole, Michelle, Toni (Donny), and my nephew Cody. To all my true friends that have been my support through this amazing journey, I love you! To Illinois Secretary, Jesse White, thank you for all your hard work for organ donation. I also thank you for giving me the opportunity to represent this cause that you are so passionate about.

To all of the nurses that work so hard in a thankless profession and take such good care of those that need you. Thank you! To Doctor Mangus and all the surgeons and doctors that work so hard for your patients. Thank you! To my donor and the donor family, who I am so grateful to. I am very cognizant of the fact that you lost a loved one, and I am so sorry. I hope to one day meet you, and I hope you take solace in knowing that your loved

one continues to live on through me! Because your loved one was

generous enough to become an organ donor… My Story Continues, and

My Story is God's Glory.

INTRODUCTION

Have you ever stared death in the eyes and been at peace with its unfriendly, cold hand? Have you ever seen the hand of God at work? Well, I have. I was on the transplant waiting list, in desperate need of a liver. It was 3:45 am on a snowy, bitter-cold, November, Saturday morning in 2007 when I received the long-awaited call. *"Can you be at the hospital within the hour? We have a liver for you,"* the male voice on the other line said, pleased to deliver the news. He paused for my answer.

"I stammered, 'Yes, of course!' My initial excitement was soon followed by a sense of panic and dread. Before I hung up the phone, shock began to set in. Although this was a long awaited call, the reality and shock of having major surgery began to set in. I had just gotten remarried, and the career I worked hard for was going well. Essentially, I had everything going for me except a significant hurdle: I had stage 4 cancer of the liver. I got the diagnosis a little less than a year prior to proposing to my newfound love. She was there with me when the doctor delivered the bad news that, without the liver transplant, I had only a short time left to live.

How could this be? I didn't feel sick. I had survived so many of life's challenges already: When I was a toddler, my mother was told that I would never walk, yet the next day I took my first steps. I was hit by a pickup truck when I was ten and walked away without a scratch. Additionally, I almost drowned in our swimming pool, narrowly missed being shot in the head when a bullet whizzed past my ear, and finally died on the operating table during a liver transplant.

Throughout my life's journey, through the good and bad, God has always made his presence known to me. He has always shown me that he cares for me, is protecting me, and is watching over me. As you read this story I hope you make this connection as well. I also hope my life will be a testimony of how great God is, and that it will bring you closer to him.

PART 1 - THE EARLY YEARS

CHAPTER ONE

THE EXPEDITION BEGINS

This journey called life is a road that every individual must travel. Along the way you will be faced with the tough decision of choosing a path to follow. What you go through to reach your destination differs for everyone.

When I was four, my family lived in an old brown brick apartment building on 101st and State Street on the South Side of Chicago, Illinois. It was me; my mother; my older brother Terrence; and my godmother, Pat. My mother was 5'3", brown complected, long haired and beautiful! She was a stern but a very loving mother. Terrence was 5'5", light complected, and my best friend and playmate with a rough and tough side. My godmother was about 5'5" with red hair and glasses, and she was white. She was also a chain smoker. Every time you saw her, she had a cigarette in her mouth.

One hot summer night in 1975, my godmother, who had just bought a brand-new Buick, was screaming out of our third floor apartment window at these dudes who were sitting on her car. "Get off of my car," she yelled down to them.

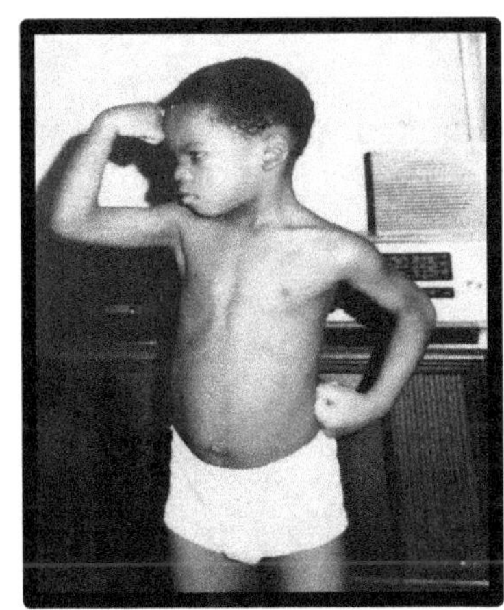

They yelled back, "Shut up, you old honkey b**ch!"

I was nosey and wanted to see what was going on, so I went to a different window and heard them telling each other to hurry up and get the hubcaps. My godmother grabbed her gun and started to head downstairs when my mother stopped her and said, "No, are you trying to go to jail over some hubcaps?" My mother then said, "We have got to move," before yelling at me, "Boy, get away from that window and go sit down!"

The next thing I remember is driving for what seemed like forever in a moving truck through the freezing cold. It was nighttime when we pulled up to the driveway of this white house with black shutters in a neighborhood that didn't look like anything on the South Side of Chicago. When I asked where we were, my mother replied, "At our new home."

I asked, "Is this still Chicago?"

My mother replied, "No, this is Streamwood."

I wasn't excited because my throat was killing me, I was burning up and I had no energy at all. I also thought that there was something off about the house, and I didn't want to live there. I got my own room, which I had mixed feelings about because my brother—who was my playmate, friend, and protector—wouldn't be in the room with me, and I would be alone. My mother began giving me different things like orange juice. I could barely get it downed because it burned my throat so bad. My mother discovered that my tonsils were infected, and that is what was causing me to be so sick. She was able to get a prescription filled in the middle of the night of penicillin, which kicked in and reduced my fever pretty quick and the Tylenol reduced the pain.

When I started to feel better, I began exploring the house which had some pretty interesting nooks and crannies in it. When you walked through the front door, there were two sets of stairs: one that led upstairs to the main level; and one that led downstairs. There was a family room to the left. The family room was pretty cool, because not only did it have a bar, but it also had this wood panel wall that opened up and laid down on the floor. To the left of that wall was a small bathroom. To the right of the family room, a long dark hallway led to the back part of the basement with one room to the right of that hallway that wasn't too scary because in the day there was a lot of sunshine from the window.

The next room down the hall was the laundry room. The laundry room had a chute from the main level, so while you were up there you could throw your dirty clothes into the chute, and it would land in a basket in the laundry room. From the front door, if you went up the stairs immediately, right in front of you was the kitchen, which had two doors. One that led outside to the back porch and the other that led to the dining room. and if you turned left, there was the front room. To the right of that was the dining room.

Down the hallway from the kitchen was a bathroom on the left, and the first bedroom to the right, which turned out to be my bedroom. At the end of the hallway were two more rooms. One room was this huge master bedroom with its own bathroom on the left. There was another large bedroom across the hallway from it. This house had a huge backyard with plenty of room to play and hang out. It also had an in-ground concrete swimming pool that went from three feet to six feet deep. Adjacent to the swimming pools was a shed to store lawn equipment. In my childlike mind, this seemed to be a good place to make a fort. The house was built on a hill, so in the farthest point in the back of the yard, behind the shed was the top of the hill. It had this weird retainer wall that went from the left of the yard all the way to the right of it. The wall was taller than the shed, so standing on top of that wall felt like standing on top of a small new kingdom. That is when I quickly learned that I am afraid of heights.

The whole yard was surrounded by a wooden gate, which was great because my mother got me a German Shepherd, I guess to ease the move. I named him John. He was brown with black tips on his ears, nose, and feet.

John was huge. I literally rode him like a horse at times, which is one of

the many ways that we played. When I explored the backyard with John, I

remember looking down at him, saying, "Well boy, we can have some

great adventures back here." John was also a great protector and fun to

play with. I just had to whistle for him, and he would be right there by my

side.

Terrence and I played around a lot. Sometimes, when I wouldn't

leave him alone, Terrence pinned me down to the ground and instead of

punching me. He would tickle me so much and so hard that it began to hurt. When that happened, I whistled for John. He would run at full speed and tackle my brother off me. One time, Terrence tried to cover my mouth so I couldn't whistle, but I was able to get half of a whistle out. John was awesome! With that half of a whistle, he came charging.

One day, as Terrence and I were outside playing, we noticed John started limping. The limping began to escalate and John eventually had trouble walking. At that point, my godmother took him somewhere. I never knew where they went or what was wrong with him, but I never saw him again after that. No matter how much I asked, I could never get an answer to what happened to John. I was pretty sad about not having him around anymore and missed my friend. I eventually got another dog, which was a gray and black miniature schnauzer named Schultzy. I tried to play with her, but we didn't bond like John and I did. Schultzy got out of the gate and ran away one night. I searched for her for hours, but I could not find her.

I never left the house much, and when I did, the furthest I traveled was the backyard. I guess that's what led to my huge imagination because I was the type of kid that could play all alone. Just give me my Hot Wheels cars and other toys, and you wouldn't have to worry too much about me. My Hot Wheels cars were my pride and joy. I would have races with spectacular crashes or acrobatic jumps that usually landed on all four wheels with my favorite car winning the race. This would usually take place throughout the house but only on the main level and never in a scary basement.

My mother and godmother tried their best to make the family room area in the basement my play area. The Christmas of 1979, I got my dream toy—an electric Hot Wheels racetrack. I also got a black and gold Schwinn BMX bicycle with off road tires. I couldn't ride my bike of course because it was the middle of winter, which left me with my racetrack, which was great. The only problem was my godmother stored the racetrack on the hide away panel wall in the family room of the basement. It was okay, I guess, as long as I had John with me, but he wasn't around anymore since that day my godmother took him with her and came back home without him.

I grew tired of playing with the racing track by myself. Although my brother Terrence was around, he was about to turn 16. His life had turned into smoking weed, hanging out with the friends that he made easily, and chasing girls. He wasn't focused on spending time with this 9 year old brother anymore. Terrence had also gotten a pet boa constrictor that was white with red eyes. My brother called me downstairs to the office in the basement. He invited me in and said he wanted to show me something cool. He shut the door and turned off the light. Within about a minute or so, he turned the light back on. I looked down because I felt something, and the snake had wrapped itself around my feet. I screamed at the top of my lungs! When I woke up, my mother was screaming at my brother, and she was cradling me calling my name. To this day, because of that moment, I still fear snakes.

My brother's childhood friend from Chicago, Fred, would come out and stay with us every other weekend. He was so cool and mellow. Fred was my knight in shining armor. He, like my brother, was someone that I looked up to. The way he spoke, the way he carried himself, and the fact that he never seemed to lose his temper the way my brother did. They were like night and day. Although Fred was great, I still wanted to spend time with Terrence. I found myself wanting more and more to have my brother's attention and time. Even though I was only 9 years old, I wanted to be with him and his friends. So I devised a plan - either my brother let me be part of his new teenage life, or I would tell mom all about his

mischievous behavior. Little did I know that the plan I devised would take

me on a wild teenage ride that I wasn't ready for.

CHAPTER TWO

NO LOVE LOST

The bond between my brother and me is special. It is

forged from an unspoken love as we grew up together,

facing life's challenges, which bonded us forever.

Terrence got his first car that Christmas. It was a green 1971 Dodge Demon with white stripes down the hood and reminded me of one of my Hot Wheels cars. The deal was my brother only had his permit and wouldn't get his license until his birthday, which wasn't until January. My mother and godmother both worked overnight at the post office, so my brother would have to watch me while they worked at night. One night my brother's friends were over at the house, which was pretty common, and I welcomed the company because they liked having me around, especially when my brother didn't.

On this particular night, my brother was in the backyard showing off his car. I heard the sound of the car being turned on and I came running out of the house. I told my brother that mom said he wasn't supposed to drive the car. He told me to shut up, to which I replied, "I am going to tell unless I can go too." I hated being in the scary house alone, and I always liked hanging out with my big brother. He told me to open the double gate, which led down the driveway. I opened the gate and closed it once he had the car out of the backyard. I stood there with a sorry look in my eye until he

Listed from left; My sister Idelle, Me, my older brother Gerald, my mother Inez, and my brother Terrence.

angrily whispered, "Come on." I jumped in the backseat with the biggest grin on my face and told my imaginary friend, and my common sense, that we would be right back. They quickly jumped in too because they did not want to be left in the scary house alone either. The devil began whispering *"this is going to be fun," while the angel said "we should not be doing this"*

My brother raced the car up and down the street and eventually we wound up in a snow- filled parking lot. My brother looked over his shoulder with a smile of mischief and said, "Hold on." He started making the car spin in circles and slide from left to right, while the engine roared. He spun the steering wheel around, making the car spin around too. We eventually wound-up sliding in full circles with everything out of the front window looking like a complete blur. The last thing I saw on one of the rotations, before being thrown to one side of the car, was a big signpost embedded in a cement block that said *No Parking*. We were heading straight for it! By this time, the angel and the devil were in an epic battle in my head. My imaginary friend was running in circles with scissors, screaming at the top of his lungs. And my common sense had decided to wander off somewhere and was MIA. At the last minute, my brother threw the car into another spin around the sign!

When we got back to the house, I could barely contain myself, my imaginary friend was beside himself with giddiness from the thrill we had just experienced, the angel and the devil were not speaking to each other, and my common sense was left speechless. My brother swore me to secrecy as he slightly grinned

Listed from left; My brother Gerald, Me, my mother Inez, my brother Terrence, and my sister Idelle.

at the pleased and excited look on my face. Of course, the next day my brother got caught because of the tracks in the snow from where the car was parked in the backyard. My brother tried to say that he did start the car and move it back and forth a little, but that he never left the backyard with it.

One thing about my mother is that she was very smart. She subtly suggested that I said I saw him take the car out of the backyard, and with that he caved and fessed up. That started the war between me and my brother, because I was labeled a snitch from that point on. Even when I tried to tell my brother and his friends that I had not said anything, no one believed me. About a week later, I found out that my brother was an avid weed head. I found his bong, which he had inadvertently left out in the open in the basement where he and his friends were hanging out. I happened to find it as my mother was coming downstairs to do laundry. I quickly picked up the bong along with the lighter and baggy with this green leafy stuff in it that smelled horrible, and hid it behind the couch.

After a few days, my mother picked up on the silent feud between me and my brother and tried to fix it by making him teach me how to swim in our in-ground pool in the backyard. My brother of course was not happy about this at all, but my mother told him he couldn't have friends over and he couldn't swim in the pool until I learned how to swim. My mother was hoping to rekindle the bond between my brother and I, but my brother didn't have a lot of patience. He tried to be patient and he tried to teach me, but I was a kid and all I wanted to do was play.

My brother had enough one day as I made him chase me around the pool. I thought it was funny to get on his nerves. Usually, he would relent and play along; however, this day he was not in the mood. My brother was fast and caught me in the yard away from the pool. He picked me up and said, "Swim," as he carried me over to the deep end of the pool and proceeded to throw me in. As I came up one of the few times for air, I not only realized that I was drowning, but that my brother was walking away and into the house!

I know angels surrounded me that day because something said to me, "Calm down, and think." I felt like I was being helped. I fished a lot as a kid and also played with frogs, and everything. Flashes of watching frogs swim came across my mind as I was sinking to the bottom of the pool and gulping water, and something said, *"Swim like you saw the frogs do and get to the side of the pool."* As I did my best frog impression, I literally felt like I was being helped to make it to the side of the pool. When I got there, I was gasping for air and crying. I was barely able to drag myself out, but when I did, I lay on my back grateful to be alive. My brother, who came back outside, saw me lying on the side of the pool and threatened me not to tell or else. He also said, "I wouldn't have let you drown. I was watching you."

I thought, *"Yeah. Right."*

A few days later, my brother was going to the store, and to run a couple of other errands. My mother told him to take me with him, and we looked at each other with disdain and disgust. Once again, my mother was a smart woman, and this was her way of making us work out our issues. My brother growled, "Why do I have to take him?"

My mother gave the typical parent answer and said, "Because I said so." Suddenly my brother lost interest in running his errands or going to the store. My mother asked, "Why don't you want to take your brother?"

My brother replied, "Because I don't want to, he gets on my nerves, and he is a snitch."

My mother smirked and asked, "What did he snitch about? Because if you are talking about you sneaking your car out, he never said a word; you told on yourself."

We wound up going, and as we got in his car, he growled, "Get in the back seat!" We went to the store and on the way home stopped and picked up a couple of his friends. As they talked and joked around, one of his friends began to ask my brother if he had any weed. My brother quickly tried to shut his friend up, saying that I was a snitch so they couldn't talk about it in front of me. His friend looked back at me and said, "You are a snitch? That's not cool."

I was already annoyed but now I was getting pissed. My imaginary friend began whispering in my ear, which I quickly repeated: "I did not tell Mom about your bong that I hid!"

My brother turned around and looked at me with confusion. He said, "I thought Mom got that and threw it away. I was wondering why she never said anything or tried to kill me. You got it?"

I said, "Yeah and the weed too!" The angel and the devil began another epic battle in my head, the devil saying, *We are drug dealers now. We can get whatever we want out of him now!* And the angel said, *No, we should tell.* My imaginary friend was screaming, *What do you think we can get?* And my common sense was in a corner, rocking, saying, *We are all going to jail like on TV!*

My brother's friends laughed with amazement and said, "Your little brother is pretty cool!" One of my brother's friends who had a little brother my age, said his little brother would have told on him as quickly as he could have. They all laughed, and my brother dropped his friends off. After an awkward silence, my brother asked, "So where did you hide it?" I told him I hid it behind the couch because Mom was coming downstairs to do laundry. After another awkward silence, he said with a tremble in his voice, "Thank you." We pulled up in front of our house and he parked.

Noticing that he hadn't driven to the backyard, I asked, 'You're not putting the car in the backyard?'

He looked at me and smiled and said, 'Nope, you are!'

I was suddenly filled with excitement and nervousness all at the same time. I asked, "What about Mom?"

"Don't worry, little bro, I got you, and this will be our secret!"

My imaginary friend smiled, my common sense strapped on his seatbelt, and the angel and the devil were silent as they both nodded their heads in agreement. My brother and I were cool again!

CHAPTER THREE

MY MORAL COMPASS STOLEN

There are many things that happen to you that you may

not be able to control, but you can decide not to be

destroyed by them.

That spring, my mother and godmother began to push me to go

outside more. The first time I took my Schwinn out, there was still a light

dusting of snow on the ground, but the weather was warm. I rode my bike

for blocks and blocks around my house, enjoying the breeze and how fast

the bike was. It peddled with such ease, and as I shifted through the gears,

it only seemed to get faster. I had never ridden a freewheel bike before, so

of course there were a couple mishaps. Like the time I was trying to hit the back brake to make the bike slide. Well, of course, I hit the front brake instead of the back, and I flipped over the handlebars. It looked like something right out of the *Three Stooges*!

Some kids saw me riding around their neighborhood and began to wonder who the new kid was. I later found out that I stuck out like a sore thumb because there were only two black families in Streamwood at the time. After I was tired of riding, I went home and put my bike up in the basement family room, which is where I was told to keep it if I wasn't riding it. A few days later, about four kids from the surrounding

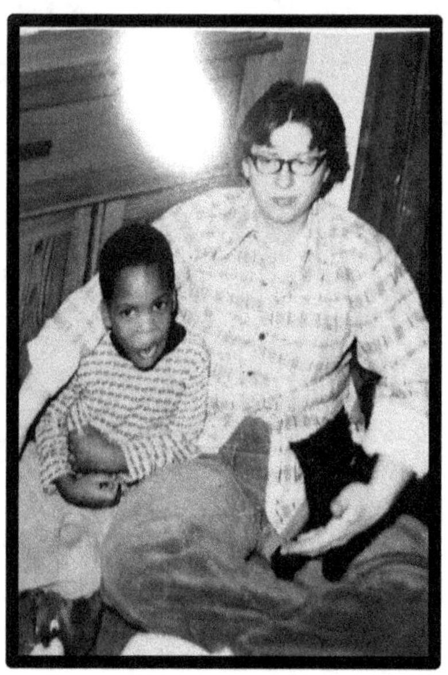

My godmother Pat and I.

neighborhood showed up on my doorstep. They rang the doorbell and my mother answered. She called me out of my room and asked me if I knew these boys, to which I replied, "No." One of the boys overheard this and spoke up to say that they would show me around the neighborhood and were hoping to become friends.

The boys asked my mother if I could come out and ride my bike with them. I didn't really want to and was very apprehensive because that would mean leaving the safety of my home. I didn't know these boys, and I was very skeptical about their true intentions. Three of the boys were my age, but the main boy, who did most of the speaking and I guess was considered the leader, was a lot older. He was really scruffy with long brown hair and looked like he had been in a fight because he had a black eye. All four of them were white, which didn't matter too much at the time because I didn't really see skin color; I just knew that they were different from me.

My mother convinced me to go ride with them. I got my bike out and we rode around for a bit before one of the boys asked the older boy, "What do you think Leslie is doing right now?"

The older boy laughed and said, "I don't know. Let's go see."

Then one of the other boys spoke up and said, "Do you think we should bring him along?"

The older boy said, "He's cool and this will be fun."

We rode to another neighborhood not too far from mine and arrived at Leslie's house. The boys walked up to the door, but because I was uncomfortable, I stayed on my bike. They rang the doorbell, and this older girl came to the door. She was average height with hazel eyes, long blonde hair and huge breasts.

"Can you come out and play?" the older boy asked, and she replied, "Play what?" With a devilish grin, he said, "Truth or Dare," and without skipping a beat she looked at me and said, "Not with him!"

I was thinking, *What is Truth or Dare*? But I said, "Don't worry about it, I'll see you guys later." I instantly felt like garbage, and I kinda got mad at myself for even going with these guys. The older boy spoke up and told me to wait a minute. He then said to Leslie, "Wow, you're like that?" To which she replied no, but that she didn't know me.

The older boy said, "I will vouch for him, he is cool," at which point Leslie said, "Give me a minute."

All four boys seemed to have gotten really excited and started talking about how great this was going to be. Leslie came out of her house and began walking with us as we slowly peddled toward a nearby forest preserve. The whole time, I stayed in the back, not knowing what was going on or what was about to happen.

We got to a point in the forest preserve where we had to walk our bikes through an overgrowth of trees. We came to what looked like a very poorly made treehouse. It had cardboard over the top of it as a roof, sticks and trees and blankets for walls, and an old carpet as a floor.

We piled our bikes up where we could see them and entered the makeshift treehouse. We all sat around in a circle, and the older boy asked me, "Have you ever played Truth or Dare?"

I said, "No, what's that?" I got kind of curious as they all sat around. I kind of giggled and laughed at the fact that I'd never heard of or played this game before.

The older boy asked Leslie to explain the game and the rules to me. She looked at me somewhat annoyed and said, "Just watch." She picked one of the other boys and said, "Truth or dare?"

He said, "Dare."

She smiled and said, "Okay."

He said, "I dare you to open your shirt."

Leslie once again looked at me and said, "Well I don't know about that."

The boys said, "You know the rules of the game, and you have to do it."

Leslie wanted everyone to turn around, but the boy that dared her. The older boy began to get frustrated, and said, "Come on, Leslie, stop stalling."

She gave a devilish grin and then opened her shirt!

All I can remember thinking was, *Wow!*

After that, Leslie said, "Okay, it's my turn." She looked at me but then picked the older boy and said, "Truth or dare?" I sat in disbelief and amazement at what was happening!

The older boy then said, "I'm giving my turn to the new kid, because he hasn't had a chance to play yet."

Leslie then complained, "You can't do that."

The older boy said, "Forget it, let's just go."

Leslie said out of frustration, "Fine, take his turn."

I nervously asked, "Truth or dare?"

She replied, "Truth."

The older boy then asked her if he could talk to her for a second and asked us to step out of the treehouse. Once again, I felt very uncomfortable, to the point where I walked over to my bike and picked it up. The older boy came out of the treehouse and asked, "You're leaving?"

To which I replied, "Yeah. I don't want to spoil your guys' fun, and she doesn't like me."

The other boys came out of the treehouse and walked toward their bikes too, the older boy turned toward Leslie and said, "See everyone's ready to leave now."

Leslie said, "Okay, come back into the treehouse."

I was halfway on my bike, and I said, "No, that's okay, you guys go ahead."

Leslie seemed relieved and said, "See? If he wants to leave, I'll stay and play with everyone else."

The older kid came over to me and tried to convince me to stay. Eventually I came back into the treehouse and told the older kid to take his turn.

He looked at Leslie and said, "Truth or dare?"

She replied, "Dare."

He said, "I dare you to let me put it in you."

She smiled and said, "Okay, but they cannot watch."

The older kid said, "Okay, everyone get out." This kid who was always calm, now seemed nervous and excited all at the same time. We left the treehouse, but the other kids were like, "Follow us," as we walked around to the back of the treehouse where you could see in through the overgrown trees, which we had to move slightly to get a good view. I couldn't believe what I was seeing.

After a few minutes, she said, "Okay, that's enough."

As they got up and started getting dressed, the older kids said, "You can come back in now."

We sat down and began playing the game again, and it was Leslie's turn. She looked at me and asked, "Truth or dare?"

I replied nervously, "Dare."

She said, "I dare you to tongue kiss me."

I was very unsure because everybody would be watching, not to mention one of her front two teeth was discolored and very dark. All the boys began pressuring me, saying I had to do it.

Leslie looked at me and said, "Have you ever tongue kissed before?"

I replied, "No."

She said, "Come on, I'll teach you."

I kept looking back at the other boys, who were staring at us like we were some kind of freaks at a circus.

Leslie grabbed me and said, "Don't worry about them, just close your eyes and do what I do." As our lips touched, she began shoving her tongue into my mouth, she then stopped and said, "Your tongue is supposed to rub with my tongue, now try again!" After a few seconds, she pushed me away and said, "Okay, that's enough."

It was now my turn, and I wanted to see more, so I asked, "Truth or dare?"

She replied, "Dare."

I was so nervous, immature, and shy that I could barely get the words out of my mouth. I said, "I want to see your body." This time, she kicked everyone out and stood in front of me and took off her clothes.

She had hair everywhere, which matched the hair on her head and her eyebrows. At that point, the boys, who were using the same area that we had used earlier, began whooping and hollering and laughing. She quickly dressed and said, "I'm ready to go." She was upset by the fact that they were watching.

The forest preserve that we were in was right behind her house, so she said she wanted to walk home alone.

The boys decided to ride back home with me to make sure that I got there, since I didn't know the neighborhood. Of course, on the way to my house we talked about the game we just played and what just happened, and that's when I found out that Leslie was 18 years old.

I was only 10 years old! The very next day, Leslie showed up at my house. I answered the door in disbelief, and she asked if I could come outside for a little while. I asked her, "How did you know where I live?" And she said that one of the other boys told her.

After hesitating and wondering if this was a good idea, I told my mom that I was going outside to play and left with Leslie. My mother, who worked nights, slept during the day, so she was in the bed half asleep and told me to be home before it got dark. As I walked with Leslie, we went to another area very close to my house that I was unfamiliar with. We talked about where I was from and how I came to live in Streamwood. We went to an open dry drainpipe, where I guess teenagers hung out because there was a lot of garbage like beer bottles, paint spray cans, and things of that nature. Once she found a clean spot in the drainpipe, she asked, "Do you want to pick up where we left off?"

I nervously said, "Okay, sure."

She said, "I want to do something a little different with you, just do what I say." She pulled my pants down and took hers off, and She climbed on top of me.

It felt very weird, but it didn't hurt, and it felt kind of good at the same time.

She said that if I felt like I had to pee or something to take it out of her because she did not want any black babies.

After a little while, she began moaning like she had a stomach ache. She was all red in the face and panting. I asked her, "Does it hurt?"

And she replied, "No, just shut up and keep going until I tell you to stop."

After she let out a deep gasp, she told me to stop. She then told me that I was a good horse, and she would be riding me more often. At the time, I didn't realize what just happened. She said that we had to keep it a secret and not to tell anyone, especially my mother, because if I told anyone we would both get in a lot of trouble.

This continued on for about a year or two. I never told anyone because I knew that if my mother were to ever find out she would have killed us both!

One time Leslie came to my house. I asked my mother if I could have a friend come into the basement to play one time, and she reluctantly agreed.

When we went down into the basement, Leslie smiled at me and said, "Looks like I made a man out of you huh?" I was embarrassed and didn't say a word.

We went into the family room where my racetrack was. I showed her my racetrack and asked her if she wanted to play, but she said, "No, those are baby toys." She sat down on the couch in the family room, exposed her breasts, and said, "Here, play with these."

I heard my mother walking around upstairs, so I started freaking out. Leslie thought it was funny, as I was begging her and saying, "Please put those up. My mother might come down here, and she'll kill me dead." Leslie let out a big sigh as she put her breasts back in her bra and pulled her shirt down.

Just then, my mother entered the room. "Who is this?" she asked.

I said, "This is my friend Leslie. She lives not too far from here."

My mother had a displeased look and said, "Okay, nice to meet you, Leslie."

This encounter with my mother made Leslie feel very uncomfortable, so she said, "I have to go, but we will play some more later."

I walked Leslie out and no sooner had the front door shut than my mother called me into the kitchen. "Why is she hanging around here?" my mother calmly asked but with a stern tone.

I said she was just a friend that I met around the neighborhood.

"How old is she?" my mother continued to question.

I said, "I don't know," because I could tell that my mother was very upset and trying to contain herself. I didn't want her to tell me that I couldn't hang out with Leslie anymore, so I downplayed it as much as I could.

My mother then asked, "She doesn't have any friends her age?"

To which I quickly replied, "I don't know," and asked if I could go play.

My mother looked at me from the corner of her eye and asked, "Are you going to play with that girl?"

I said, "No, I am just going to play around the house."

She said, "Well, I think that girl should hang around kids her age!"

I continued playing with Leslie, just not around the house. Everything was great, until my brother began questioning me about what was going on and why I was hanging around with this girl close to his age.

Always trying to impress my brother, I told him about the game of Truth or Dare. Fred happened to be in town for the week and began teasing me and telling me that I was lying. My brother and Fred wanted me to prove what I was saying was true, and I didn't even tell them about the horse game.

They told me to go get her and bring her to the shed in the backyard of our house and play Truth or Dare with her. Because I wanted to impress them both, I went and got one of my friends and took Leslie to the shed. Before we could even get started with the game, my brother and Fred busted in. They kicked me and my friend out and told Leslie to stay. When I began to argue and protest, my brother threatened me and said, "Get out or I will kick your butt and then tell Mom."

With no other choice, we left the shed. They asked Leslie to open her shirt and began fondling her breasts. I was very angry and hit the shed, which was metal, so it made a lot of noise. This caused Leslie to jump up, close her shirt, and run out of the shed. My brother and Fred were pissed off, but I didn't care.

It wasn't too long after that that Leslie said she didn't want to do this anymore, and that she had a boyfriend. I felt used, guilty, and like I did something wrong. I had an idea that what had been happening wasn't right, but I was so confused! I didn't know if I wanted it to stop, because I felt special, and she was nice to me in a way. But at the same time, I felt guilty for what was happening. Feeling rejected, used, and hurt, I started to see this girl around Leslie's neighborhood who seemed to take a liking to me.

After talking together and hanging out for a little bit, she began to open up and tell me she really liked me. She was my age with red hair, short with a nice, developed body for her age. We would go to the makeshift treehouse and talk, hang out, kiss, and play around.

One particular day, we were in the treehouse kissing when she stopped me and said, "My dad told me never to let a nigger put anything inside of me." I stopped dead in my tracks because I was again hurt and confused.

She went on to say that her dad didn't want me hanging around her anymore because I was a nigger, so if we were going to hang out, it would have to be a secret. I remember thinking, *Another secret?*

At that point, I was ready to go. Still stunned and in shock, I walked her home. When we got to her house, her father was on the porch. He gave me a look like he wanted to kill me, and she turned to me and said I should just go. The next time I saw her, she said she couldn't speak to me or hang out with me anymore.

On the way home, I walked down this main road because my house was right off of it. As I was walking along, a car was speeding past with about four white boys in it. One of them was hanging out of the window. He screamed, "nigger," and threw a bottle at me.

I was so angry that I picked a bottle up and threw it at the car, screaming back, "F@*k you!" The bottle hit the car, and the driver slammed on the brakes and threw the car into reverse. I knew I was outnumbered, and they were much older and bigger than me, so I chose to run. They chased me until I headed into the forest preserve where Leslie had taken me before.

As they lost me in the trees, one threw a rock at me and said, "Yeah, you better run, nigger." Then they climbed back into the car and sped off.

My brother got a new car which he loved more than the Dodge Demon. He got an orange 1973 Chevy Nova with chrome mag rims. He worked on that car night and day. He even taught me how to work on it while he swapped the original engine out for a 350-horse powered engine with a Holley 4-barrel carburetor.

One day my brother and I were arguing and he threw my bike in the deep end of the pool and told me to go get it…. Later, he left with friends, so I found the car keys to that '73 Chevy Nova. I climbed into his car and started it up, but I couldn't get it into gear. My brother came back home and caught me sitting in the driver's seat revving the engine and struggling with the gear shift. He screamed for our mother while grabbing the keys, turning the engine off, and snatching me out of the car.

He told my mother what I was doing, and she said, "I thought that was you out here working on your car! My mother yelled at me, asking what the hell I was doing!

I looked up at her and said calmly, "He threw my bike into the pool and told me to go get it, so I was trying to drive his car into the pool so I could tell him to go get his car!"

My mother and brother stood there speechless. My mother was so angry she was calm. She looked at my brother and asked, "Why would you throw his bike into the pool?" Before he could answer, she screamed, "Go get his bike now!" As I smirked at him, she looked at me, not knowing what to do. She growled at me, "Do you know you could have killed yourself? What is wrong with you?"

She began yelling at me. "You would have drowned in his car trying to get revenge! JUST GO TO YOUR ROOM!" As I was walking away, my brother showed up in the driveway with my bike. His clothes were drenched.

He handed me my bike, saying, "Here, dummy! You are so stupid; you could have killed yourself! Dumbass!"

I went to my room like I was told, feeling vindicated but dumb. I was thinking to myself, *At least I made my point, don't mess with me!* But at the same time, I had not thought about the fact that, had I gotten the car into gear and driven it into the pool, I could easily have been trapped. I didn't know how to swim, and that meant I would have been stuck in the car at the bottom of our swimming pool or drowned trying to get out of the car. I got scared, because I felt myself slipping away into a darkness. The anger I felt was foreign to me. It was like crawling through a window into the unknown, or at least into what was not known to me.

CHAPTER FOUR

DESTRUCTIVE ENERGY

Who you are may be attacked, humiliated, and cruelly

ridiculed, but who you are can never be taken away

unless you give it away.

I started school that fall, and I dreaded it because I did not know
what to expect. I already had so much negativity just because of my skin
color that I knew I didn't fit in. There were four older boys that chased me
home from school on a regular basis. I never said a word to them to make
them chase me; they just said they were going to kick my black butt. My
brother happened to be outside one day and stopped me and asked me if I
was running from the boys behind me. I replied, "No, we are just playing."

The boy that was doing all of the talking said, "No, we are not playing. We are going to kick his black butt."

My brother, who was a star running back on the football team, was all muscle. A lot of people were afraid of him. He didn't care who you were; he demanded respect. During one of his games, he was tackled, and they piled on him. There was a loud scream of pain. Jersey number 58 pulled the helmet off of this other kid and hit him in the face with it, then punched him with his fists until the team pulled him off. The kid was unconscious. Then number 58 was being helped off of the field. It looked like his ankle was broken. My mother grabbed her things and yelled, "Come on, baby." Number 58 was my brother! My brother asked the boy why the other kids behind him were there and if they were going to fight me too.

He said, "Yeah, we are all going to kick his butt."

My brother said, "All of you are not going to fight my brother."

So the main guy said, "I don't need them. I will kick his butt."

My brother told everyone to come into our backyard behind the shed, and me and the main guy were going to fight.

We are? I thought.

I said to my brother, "I don't want to fight."

He replied, "You are not going to embarrass me. You are going to fight him, or you will have to fight me!" There was no way I wanted to fight my brother; he was crazy. When he was teaching me how to fight, he would do things to try to make me mad because I wouldn't fight. He made me so mad one time that I hauled off and punched him in the mouth. His head jerked backward, and I thought, *Oh man, why did I do that? I am about to die.* He looked at me and smiled and licked the blood from his busted lip. He said, "That's what I am talking about."

I was convinced then, if I wasn't before, that he was nuts. This is the same person that, when my mother forced him to babysit me, went outside and had a snowball fight with some girls that stopped by the house. I beat on my bedroom window, whining and making faces at him while pressing my face against the window because I wanted to go outside too. He got mad and threw a snowball at the window so hard that it shattered with my face pressed up against it. Blood was everywhere, and my face was cut up. The girls ran to my aid while my brother kept saying, "He's okay." Then he told me to stop faking.

We gathered behind the shed, and that's when I found out that the boy lived right behind my house. His brother saw all of us gathered behind the shed and came over, asking what was going on. My brother explained what happened, and that we were going to fight it out one on one. His older brother wasn't happy with his little brother because he didn't feel the same way. My brother told everyone that if anyone tried to jump in, he would get involved.

I stood there not knowing what to do when the kid came at me swinging. I dodged his punches and countered with a couple of hits to the body and one to his jaw. He fell backward on the ground, and before he could get back up, I was on top of him, wrapping him up with my right hand on the back of his head and my left arm under his left arm, pushing upward on his elbow. His older brother moved toward me, and my brother hit him so hard that we heard a very loud crack—so hard that everyone else jumped and stepped back. One of the other kids that was chasing me said he didn't even really have a problem with me and tried to leave, but my brother said, "No, stay here, nobody leaves until this is over!"

The older brother, who was bleeding from his face, said, "I was just going to break it up."

My brother looked at me and asked, "Are you all finished?"

I asked the kid, "Do you give up?"

And he responded, "F you, nigger."

I pushed up on his elbow, and the kid screamed out in pain. I didn't want anyone to hear him, so I pushed his face into the dirt pile that was by his head to muffle his screams.

He started yelling, "I give up, I give up."

I said, "Are you going to leave me alone?"

He screamed, "Yes."

For some reason, I told him to eat the dirt by his head. He started eating the dirt like it was his favorite dessert.

My brother said, "Okay, that's enough, get off of him." I got up and the kid got up, looking at me like this wasn't over while he was holding his arm and crying.

My brother asked the older brother, "Are we cool?"

The kid's older brother said, "Yeah, we are cool."

When they left, the older brother started scolding his brother, asking why he was messing with me and where he got that prejudice stuff from.

The kid said that their father talked about blacks in that way. The older brother said, "And you are stupid enough to listen to Dad? You are a dumb ass!!"

The police came to the house as the fight ended, saying that they heard there was a problem with some kids chasing me. My brother, who knew the police very well and was even sleeping with the female officer that showed up for this call, told the officer, "There is no problem. I handled it. It's done."

The female officer smirked at my brother and said, "Terrence, what did you do?"

My brother said, "Don't worry about it, let's just say they won't be chasing him anymore."

Some boys that I thought were cool asked me to come check out their fort and hang out. They had a girl with them, and I thought about Leslie. I was curious, so I went. They smoked cigarettes on the way to their fort and tried to get me to smoke too. As soon as we got to the fort, we started playing Truth or Dare. The girl picked me to go first, and of course I picked dare. She dared me to show her my thing. When I unzipped my pants, the boys grabbed me and started trying to get my pants off. They were talking about taking turns doing me in the butt, and the girl wanted to watch! I fought to keep my pants on, but not before they wrestled me to the ground where they took turns putting their cigarettes out on my butt. They got up laughing, while the girl said, "I didn't even get a good look at it, aren't they supposed to have big things?"

They all started taunting me, saying, "Come on, show us, we aren't going to do anything. We just want to see it."

Of course, I left, and as I was walking away, they started calling me nigger, and told me I was being a p@**!. I didn't want to hang out with those kids anymore and I wanted to make new friends who weren't misbehaving. Over the summer, I met a kid named David in the neighborhood. He seemed to be cool and when anyone gave me crap because of my skin color, he was quick to stand up for me. David was white with red hair and freckles, and he was very hyper. He told me that he would be going to the same school I would be going to, so we could hang out every day.

I also met a kid named Jeff, who was cool too. I would spend nights at their houses during sleepovers. Even though it took me out of my comfort zone, it was fun! My brother was friends with the next-door neighbor, his name was Frank, and he was a Vietnam veteran. He was loud, and intimidating, but fun. He was tall with a very muscular build, and he had a temper. He had a wife who was quiet and didn't really speak to anyone. They had a daughter who was my age named Crystal. She was very pretty. She was short with long brown hair and full lips with a nice shape. She was very bossy but nice.

I walked to school alone every day, and I hated it because everyone, from adults to kids, would stare at me like I was an alien while they whispered and pointed. One day a group of girls I walked past started calling me a monkey and making fun of me. Out of nowhere, Crystal started yelling at the girls, telling them to leave me alone and that what they were saying wasn't right. For someone so short, she had a set of lungs on her. The main girl that was taunting me told Crystal to shut up and asked if I was her pet monkey. Crystal threw her book bag down on the ground and got in the girl's face, threatening to kick her butt.

The girl backed down, but Crystal took it a step further and told her to apologize to me. To my amazement, she reluctantly apologized. Crystal picked up her book bag and walked up to me and said, "Hurry up, you are going to be late for school!"

She went back to walking with her friends, and I could hear some of them telling her she did the right thing, and that the girl was a bitch. Her other friends asked, "Why did you do that?"

Crystal answered by asking them, "What if that was you? How would you feel? It's not right!"

It didn't get any better when I got to school. I met the only other black person there, who was a girl. She was average height with a beautiful dark complexion. She had long hair and a smile that made my knees weak. Her name was Michelle.Unfortunately, when I spoke, she looked at me like I was something she stepped in and told me to never speak to her again. She treated me worse than the other kids that called me names.

Every day I was reminded that I was a nigger, and I was not as good as the other kids in the school. I tried out for the school basketball team and made it. I was taller than the rest of the kids so that might have had something to do with it, but either way I made the team! My coach's name was Coach Harland. He was 6'7" with curly brown hair and a mustache. I found out from my brother that he was a former basketball player. I asked Coach Harland about it, and he was quick to show me pictures from when he played in high school and college. My first game, Coach Harland put me in. I really had no idea what I was doing; all I knew was to get the ball and pass it off to someone that was open for the shot. I got a rebound but instead of passing it off, I began to dribble down court. I had an open shot, so I put it up while Coach Harland screamed, "No!"

I missed the shot, and the other team got the rebound and scored. During the next practice, Coach was going over some plays and basics with me. Frustrated, he got face to face with me and said, "I never met a nigger that couldn't play basketball." I later quit the team. I went silent; I wanted to be alone. I didn't have the words to even vocalize how I felt. My being was shrunk and filled with a sense of somberness. This somberness came from feeling like an outcast even more than I already did. No matter how hard I tried to fit into this little town, called Streamwood, nothing seemed to work.

CHAPTER FIVE

THE DARKNESS OF THE STORM

When Darkness drives you to the end of your rope, do

everything you can to cling to hope.

Father's Day rolled around, and we had to do these artistic Father's Day projects. I didn't have a father; my mother was all I knew. I didn't know my father's name, what he looked like, or where he was.

I whispered my dilemma to the teacher, and she blurted out loud, "You don't have a father?"

I quickly looked around the room as I heard the snickering, and everyone was staring at me. I answered her with a muttered no.

She then asked, "Do you have a mother?"

I didn't answer.

She then said, "Well make one for your mother then or just sit there."

I had never thought of my father before.

I became very angry from that day forward. I was mad at the teacher for embarrassing me. I was tired and mad at all the kids relentlessly making fun of me; and I was pissed off that I didn't have a father like everyone else. At twelve years old I just became angry at life. I began to pay attention and saw kids doing fun things with their fathers, like fishing, camping, or even just playing catch. I felt myself changing. I went from this quiet, naïve boy, who used to make up songs about the Lord and sing them to God, to this anger-filled boy who was pissed off at the world.

I began acting out at school, starting with the teacher that embarrassed me. I became an extremely disrespectful smart-ass and gave her a really hard time. A lot of the kids really liked the teacher and tried sticking up for her, but I started scaring some of them with my temper and my lack of respect for anyone or anything. Like I thought about my brother, they thought I was nuts! While I was in the bathroom, three of the boys from my classroom confronted me. They said that I needed to know my place and that maybe they should remind me that I was just a nigger. I remembered what my brother said about taking out the leader of the group first, and with that I grabbed the main one by the back of his head and rammed his face into the bathroom wall. I yelled back, "Maybe I should remind you that I don't give a f@*k, and I will f@*k you all up if you keep messing with me!"

The other two grabbed the main one, who was ready to fight me, and told him not to fight there, but they could catch me after school. They said, "You better run because we're going to beat your butt after school." Then they left the bathroom.

At the end of the day, I heard the three boys speaking with the teacher, telling her, "It's okay, don't worry about it, we're going to teach him a lesson." The teacher nodded and she looked at me and then down at the ground.

The boys walked past me, saying, "Yeah, we're going to have some fun."

I walked down the path that led from the school and started feeling a little overconfident because I didn't see the boys anywhere in sight.

Once I got to the street, there were a whole bunch of kids gathered on the other side, which was not normal. I lived on that side of the street so I had to walk through the crowd in order to get down the street to my house. As I got to the other side of the street, I saw the three boys waiting for me. I kept walking as they started following and taunting me. One of them punched me, and that's when I swung back, punching one of them in the mouth. The main boy yelled at the other two, saying, "Get his arms!" As they struggled to grab me, the main one started to punch me like he was punching a punching bag. Trying to get away, I tried to drop down and slide out of their grip, but it didn't work, and I wound up on the ground on my back with the other boys still holding my arms.

After a few more punches, one of the boys that was holding me said, "Let me get a turn." The main boy went to grab me while the other boy let go, but once my arm was free, I began fighting back again. They all stood up and started kicking and stomping on me. As I tried to get to my feet, they picked up rocks and threw them at me. I charged the main boy to try to knock him down so I could get on top to punch him. But when I stood up to charge him, I got hit in the head with a rock, which made me dizzy so I kind of fell into him.

He threw me toward the curb where there was a parked car, and I hit my head on its bumper. As I lay there bleeding and trying to get back up to fight, Crystal popped up with her friends as well as some grown-ups who were driving past and pulled over to break up the crowd that had gathered for the fight. Crystal and her friends helped me to my feet. Crystal thanked her friends and the adults that pulled over and told them, "You guys go ahead, I got him from here." Limping home, I tried to hold it together as best as I could in front of Crystal, who was doing her best to help me walk, but halfway there I couldn't hold it together anymore. I broke down. I was so angry and so confused. I was angry because I lost the fight with the three boys, but at the exact same time I was so confused and frustrated because I couldn't understand how I could be disliked so much simply because of my skin color.

Crystal said, "Some people are just stupid, just ignore them," as she began to cry too. When we got home, my mother asked what happened to me, but I wouldn't answer her. I just stared down at the ground in shame and frustration. Crystal explained everything that took place from the teacher embarrassing me to the kids threatening me in the bathroom. Then she gave a very detailed account of the fight. While my mother and godmother tended to my wounds, my godmother, who was very hot-tempered, told me what to do the next time something like that happened.

My godmother said, "Pick up a brick, a tree branch, anything and beat them in the head with it."

My mother began arguing with her and told me, "No. don't do that." She said that I should defend myself the best way I could or run if I had to, but that if I listened to my godmother I would wind up in jail. My mother said, "You're black, so the rules are different for you. You can't do the same things that they do and get away with it." She also told me to NEVER hang my head in shame.

My brother, who was beyond angry, tried to make me feel better. He said, "They couldn't take you one-on-one little brother. They had to gang up to get you."

I played sick for about a week after that incident, not because I was scared to go back to school, but because I didn't want to deal with the crap that I would have to deal with for losing the fight. Even though it was three on one, I was done dealing with the way I was being treated. That weekend, my mother and godmother loaded me and my brother into the car and we drove an hour and thirty minutes out to the middle of nowhere. We pulled up to this building on this huge campus that looked like a college. We went inside and it turned out to be a school.

We took a tour, and the place had it all. It had a gym that made the gym at my school look tiny. It had a cafeteria with all different types of food and a machine where you could get anything you wanted to drink, from juice to soda. We went outside, and I saw this huge playground where older kids with remote control cars were racing each other, while other kids played catch with a football. On another part of the playground was a basketball court, and they even had a baseball field. They had kids that were younger than me as well as my age. They also had kids that looked like they were my brother's age, which made me think to myself, *"Wow, Terrence will have fun here!"* There were girls there as well, from younger than me up to girls that looked my brother's age. One of them smiled at my brother and gave a flirtatious wave.

My brother waved back and gave a look like he liked what he saw. We went to another part of the building where they had all of these bunk beds. It kind of looked like the barracks from one of my favorite TV shows called *Mash*.

That's when I heard the person giving us the tour say, "And this is where the boys stay, and the girls stay in the dorms on the other side of the campus."

We headed to the office, where we sat down with this man from the school who gave us this tour. He smiled at me and asked, "So what do you think of the school?"

I said, "It's nice." I then looked at my brother and said, "What do you think, do you like it?"

My brother replied, "Yeah, but you are the one that will be going here, what do you think?"

My mouth instantly got dry, and I said, "NO!" as I waited for someone to tell me it was a joke and that my brother would be attending this school and not me.

My mother spoke up and said, "You don't want to go here?"

I thought, *HELL NO!* but what came out of my mouth was, "I would have to stay here?"

The man from the school said, "Well, we do have daytime students that go home every day, but you would stay here Monday through Friday, and you would only go home on the weekend if your mother came to get you."

I got highly upset and looked at my mother and blurted out, "I don't want to stay here!"

After getting some papers from the man, my mother thanked him. The man looked at me and said, "I hope you will give the school a chance."

I protested all the way to the car, and I was dead silent on the ride home. Everyone tried to comfort me by offering to get me Jack n The Box which was like McDonald's today, but I just shook my head no. They tried to take me to Toys R Us, but I refused to get out of the car. My brother began whispering to me to stop being a wimp, to which I replied with a middle finger. Everyone knew I was beyond pissed off, including my brother, who was so shocked at my response to him that he just left me alone. My brother knew I was afraid of him, so for me to respond the way I did caught him completely off guard, but it told him how angry I was.

My mother tried to reason with me and asked me what we should do. I didn't necessarily want to stay in Streamwood anymore, but I knew I didn't want to be at a boarding school. I didn't have an answer, and without an answer I could not lay out any choices to argue with. With nothing left to say, my mom signed the paperwork and I had to start school the following week.

CHAPTER SIX

ALONE AND FAR FROM HOME

Don't hide in the shadows of anger, remember to hold

on to God's hand and remind yourself that you are his

child.

That next weekend my bag was packed, and we were in the car heading back to that school. I hadn't said much, remaining silent all week unless forced to speak. I thought to myself, *why even ask me if I want to go to this place if you already had your mind made up, and my opinion didn't matter?* I felt like I was being thrown away, like by sending me to this school, I would be out of the way and forgotten about.

Everyone would take turns during the ride there trying to tell me the bright side of going to this school. That only made me look at every negative aspect, which of course I kept to myself, because I wasn't speaking to anyone. What difference would it have made anyway? When we arrived, I was shown to my bunk area where I would put my belongings. My brother, mother, and godmother helped me unpack, while I sulked and remained silent. They didn't stay long and tried to hug me and tell me how much they would miss me. I remained silent while I gave partial hugs and mean stares.

My mother, with tears in her eyes, said, "So you are not going to say anything to me, and give me that sorry hug?" It was not often that I disrespected my mother, but this was a time that I couldn't help the way I felt. I just stared at her until she said, "Okay, Phillip, I am about to go." As she got a few steps away, I ran up to her and hugged her with everything I had. My mother hugged me back and asked me to promise to just give the school a chance.

I didn't answer at first, but she kept asking with tears in her eyes. I finally responded, "Okay."

She kissed me and told me she loved me, and I told her I loved her too, and with that she left. I watched out of the window as they got in the car and drove away. Once they were out of eyeshot, a counselor came in and asked me to come and meet the other kids. Still filled with anger, I responded, "I don't want to."

She walked over to me as I sat on my bunk and sat next to me. She began trying to relate to me and telling me how the school wasn't so bad and how I could go home on the weekends. I guess she didn't know that in my mind no one was coming to get me every weekend. She eventually got me to go with her to meet the other kids, not because I wanted to, but because she was getting on my nerves and the only way to get her to leave me alone was to meet everyone. As I met the other kids, I began to notice that, once again, there were none that looked like me.

It was during the day, so the play area was coed and had girls and boys in it. They had ping-pong tables, air hockey, and pool tables. I walked over to the pool table to watch a game going on. When it ended, I tried to challenge the winner, but the kid that just lost looked at me and said, "No, I am playing again." He looked at me with his face twisted up, like I was something he found on the bottom of his shoe. The angry alter ego that began to develop because of everything I had been through up until this point, wanted to take the pool cue in my hand and smash it across the top of his head.

Wanting to smash this pool cue across this boy's head made me reflect on a situation that happened before I came to this school. The week before I left to come to this school, a kid claiming to be my friend came over to my house saying he was coming by to check on me and wanted to hang out. My mother invited him in, and I took him to the family room in the basement. We played with my Hot Wheels racing track, and he kept losing. I played with this thing so much that I knew the track inside and out as well as the cars. One of the cars, which was my favorite, I took apart to clean and tweaked. I changed the part that made contact with the track so that it would pull more electricity and make it faster.

This kid lost several races and didn't want to play anymore, so I asked if he wanted to play something else. He started going through my toy chest and started saying things like "You got an Evil Knievel? You got Mattel Electronic Football?"

He began to play with my electronic football game as I watched. He lost and threw the game on the ground out of frustration. This caused me to yell at him as I picked up the game to see if it was broken.

He responded by punching me, so I grabbed him and wrestled him down on the couch getting a couple of punches in return.

He yelled, "Get off of me you stupid nigger!"

I got up and walked over to the bar where we had a phone. I turned and faced him, while behind my back, I took the receiver off of the hook and unplugged the cord. I said, "What did you say?"

As he got up off the couch, he said, "Nothing."

I said, "No, repeat what you said!"

Without hesitation he looked at me and began to repeat what he said. In a lower voice, he said, "I said, 'Get off me you stupid—'" but before he could get the word out, I cracked him in the head with the phone receiver.

He went to yell out in pain, but before he could get a scream out, I tackled him to the floor and covered his mouth.

While sitting on his chest, I whispered, "Don't you ever call me that again or I will F you up! Do you understand?"

Not being able to speak with my hand over his mouth, he shook his head yes. I calmly got off him and said, "Okay, so now that we understand each other, what do you want to play?"

He looked at me like I was insane and said, "I want to go home."

I said, "You are ready to go so soon?"

He said, "Yeah, I just want to go home."

I looked at him with a menacing look and said, "Okay, but you are not going to tell my mom about what happened here, right?"

He looked at me with a look of fear and confusion and shook his head no.

I said, "Okay, let me walk you to the door."

I walked him out and went to my room. I was so confused because that was so far out of the norm for me. Half of me felt very guilty for what just took place, but at the same time the other half of me felt a justified feeling I hadn't experienced before, I stood up for myself and it felt good. That day I believe is when this alter ego came to the surface. My natural personality is to put others first and consider other people's feelings. My natural personality would never do something like that. But this alter ego is filled with anger and looks to protect me and think of myself first over others.

Thinking back to that day, I tried to make the best of the current situation. Instead of smashing the pool cue over this kid's head, I went over to this other area where there was a TV which had my favorite cartoon on. Just as I sat down to watch, the counselors began calling us because it was time to eat dinner. I slowly walked over and joined the others, but one of the counselors seemed annoyed with me, saying, "Go back over and turn the TV off."

The TV was already on when I went over to it the first time, and I didn't even know how to change the channel, let alone turn it off. After staring at the counselor for a second with the same attitude that she was giving me, I walked back over to the TV.

After I'd been trying to find the power button for a few minutes, this little girl ran up and said, "I can help you, the power button is here." I hit the power button and thanked the little girl, who excitedly said, "You are welcome," before skipping back over to where the others were gathered.

I slowly walked back over to the others, and we went to the cafeteria. When we got there you had to get a tray and get in line. I got a tray and got in line, where I was served meatloaf, mashed potatoes and gravy. To drink, instead of the fountain drink machine, we had a choice of regular milk or chocolate. I later found out that the fountain machine hadn't worked in a long time, and there was no idea on when it would be fixed. I looked for a place to sit in this crowded lunchroom, but everyone seemed to be grouped up. Every table that had a place to sit I was either told "Someone is sitting there," or "You can't sit here." I thought, *Different school, same old crap!* " Finally, someone at this one table motioned me over and said, "You can sit with us."

This one kid at the table did not want me sitting with them. He was Italian and his name was Frank. When I first walked up, I heard him complaining to the other kids at the table. "Why did you call him over here?"

I sat down and began to eat. As I was eating, Frank began telling me a little about himself. Then he started asking me questions about myself, which I vaguely answered.

He then asked me a question that set the tone of the relationship between us, which was "Hey, do you know what a moulinyan is?"

I stared at him intently and said, "No."

Everyone at the table started to laugh with Frank as he replied, "That's you, you are an eggplant, a moulinyan!"

Every day thereafter I sat at this table. After the first day, the counselors thought it would be a great idea to assign these as our permanent seats. I had to sit with Frank and what I called the rest of the kids at this table, Frank's audience, as he cracked jokes about me being black. After a couple of days with this, I took Frank's audience and turned the tables on him. One day while he was doing his daily routine, I cracked a couple of jokes back at him that made him very angry. Angry enough to fight.

He said, "I am going to the dentist in the morning, but tomorrow night I am going to kick your butt you moulinyan!"

The next day I looked for Frank all day, asking his friends where he was and everything. That night at dinner, Frank was there. He didn't like the fact that I was looking for him and he started challenging me right there in the lunchroom. He kept daring me to punch him in the jaw, and I declined, not wanting to get in trouble, still being new to the school and all. He began insulating me, taunting me, and daring me to punch him. Finally, my cup ran over with rage, and I punched him in the jaw with everything I could muster up. His head snapped back like he had whiplash, but after a second or two, he looked at me and smiled. He started in again, but with kind of a slurred speech, saying, "I told you guys he was a wuss; he is weak like all moulinyans. You are nothing!"

I began questioning myself because I knew I'd hit him hard as hell! I said, "Whatever, Frank," as I got up and walked away.

The next day, Frank was not at school again. The following day, he showed up with his mouth wired shut. It turns out that I broke his jaw, and the reason he didn't feel it was because he was still under the influence of the Novocain shot that he'd just had from the dentist. With no one around, Frank came over to me while I was in my bunk, which is where I went to be alone, and that was quite often. To my amazement, he apologized to me. I was taken back by the apology and slow to accept it, but I did. He walked away and left me conflicted and confused.

That was the first time anyone apologized for the way they treated me.

At dinner that night, I walked in with a different attitude than usual. I sat down at the table, and the other kids began repeating some of the things that Frank was saying before I got there. It seems that Frank had to protect his reputation when the word was going around that I broke his jaw. Frank denied that I broke his jaw and said that the reason his mouth was wired shut was because he had more dental work done. Frank looked at me, and through his teeth he said, "He didn't break my jaw; he's just a mouli, right, moulinyan?"

As I stared at him, I started thinking about all of the things I wanted to do to him. He kept up with the same bull he was doing before he apologized. The only difference was, this time, he had a look of concern on his face. I couldn't tell if it was a look of fear that I would kick his butt, or if he was worried that I would tell everyone about his fake attempt at an apology. Either way I let it go.

Every day after dinner we were given a candy bar of our choice. The counselor that I first encountered on my first day that pushed me to meet everyone, was handing out the candy bars that particular day. As she gave the candy bars out, she said that there was a charity for less fortunate kids and asked if I would like to donate my candy bar to the charity instead of eating it. Before I really had a chance to think about it, the angry side of me came out and said, "No." She said that almost all of the other kids gave their candy bars up for the charity and asked if I was sure.

I said, "I am eating my candy bar."

As I bit into it, she said to me, "I would have thought, out of all people, you would have given your candy bar up for the less fortunate."

After already taking a bite, I began to analyze what she had said. I wondered exactly what she meant by that statement. Did she mean because I was black that I would sympathize with the less fortunate?

I went back to her and asked, "Did you say anything to any of the other kids that didn't give their candy bars to charity?"

She said, "No."

I said, "So why did you say something to me?"

"Because I just thought that you would be able to understand, because you probably know some less fortunate people."

I was conflicted once again, because half of me felt bad for kids that couldn't enjoy a candy bar because they were less fortunate. But then again, I was angry because I was once again being singled out because of my color. I offered my candy bar, but it was too late because I had already opened it and bitten it. She guilted me relentlessly before telling me to go eat my candy bar, and that she didn't like selfish kids like me. As I ate my guilt-filled candy bar, I overheard her talking to the other counselors about how much fun she was having laying the guilt trip on me and playing mind games.

I didn't get much sleep at this school. Especially after one night while I was sleeping on my stomach in the top bunk.

I woke up to the bunk shaking like somebody was climbing up the side of it. Before I knew what was happening, one of the older kids was on top of me, pushing me down on my back with his arm while pulling down my pajamas with his other hand.

He had got my pajamas halfway down when I began to squirm and yell out. He said, "Shut up and just let it happen."

There was no way in hell I was going to let this or anything like it happen. Just as he began lying on top of me and trying to push himself into me, I threw my head backward, hitting him in the face. He yelped and yelled out in pain, I twisted my body sideways and got away from him.

I turned to face my attacker to see blood everywhere! I had caught him in the nose with the back of my head. He said, "I'll be back; it's going to happen."

I looked around for the counselors who were nowhere in sight. From that night on, I slept on my back and became a light sleeper. I still sleep lightly to this day. For several nights after that I could hear muffled screams and outcries, and all I kept thinking was, *Where are the damn counselors?* He never came back to my bunk, thank God! It turned out that the counselors were not doing their job at all. Some of the teenagers managed on several nights to sneak out and over to the girls' campus.

There was this one teenager who I actually thought was pretty cool and I admired. He was black, and his name was Anthony, but everyone called him Tony. He appeared on a few episodes of this TV show called *Hill Street Blues,* which was very popular at the time. He told me and some of the other kids and teenagers about the adventures he had at the female campus.

One night it was late and all you heard was loud moaning, grunting, and screams of pain.

It turned out it was Anthony, and when the counselors went to see what was going on, they found Tony in the bathroom in tears. They asked Tony what was wrong. He yelled out, "It burns and hurts, and I can't pee!" Tony had to go to the ER that night. The next day he explained that he'd caught the clap. I had no clue what the clap was, but I did know I didn't want it. Tony was expelled from the school a few days later. Not only did he catch the clap, but he got the girl that gave it to him pregnant.

To my surprise, my godmother came to get me every weekend, and every weekend, I was dead silent unless forced to speak. My godmother tried everything she could to get me to talk and loosen up. But the harder she tried, the more I ignored her. When I got home, it would be straight to my room, and I wouldn't come out unless I had to use the bathroom or eat. One time, my mother and godmother asked what they could do, and I said, "Let me come home."

My mother replied, "You are going to that school."

I was sitting on my bed, I jumped up and grabbed the mattress and threw it across the room after she left my doorway. I slammed my door shut and tore up the entire room. I had all of this pent-up rage, hate, and anger inside of me that boiled over.

My mother pushed my door open when I was done and said, "Boy, have you lost your mind? Clean it up now!"

One weekend it was snowing like I had never seen it snow before. It was nonstop, thick, and heavy. The counselor kept telling me that my godmother probably wouldn't be coming and to start preparing to stay for the weekend. All the other kids had been picked up, and I would have been the only kid staying. I stared out of the window like a lost puppy, hoping and praying that she would show up. I had begun to give up hope, and the counselor had already called the office to say they had one kid that weekend. Then I saw a car coming down the long winding driveway, and my hope skyrocketed again.

All you could see were the headlights because of the thick snow coming down, but as the car got closer, my wishes and prayers were answered. It was my godmother! I looked at the counselor with a smug look and grabbed my bag. She told me to wait because my godmother had to come in and sign me out. That was the first time in two months that I spoke and conversed with my godmother. I was so happy that she showed up that I was able to put aside all the anger for the time being. It took forever to get home, but we made it.

The next day there was so much snow that literally there was a snowdrift that went to the roof of our house. The day was a lot of fun; my brother grabbed me and threw me into the air, and I landed in a snowdrift that my brother had to dig me out of. My godmother used a snowdrift to climb to the roof of our house. Then she skied off the side of the house. I later found out that they called that snowstorm the blizzard of 1979. Neither my mother nor my godmother took me back to that school after that weekend. I was elated that I didn't have to return to that, horrible godforsaken school. However, unbeknownst to me there was a new adventure

on the horizon.

PART 2 - GROWING PAINS

CHAPTER SEVEN

WELCOME TO CHI-TOWN

No matter how hard the past is, you can always begin again. Every day is a chance to begin again. Don't focus on the failures of yesterday; start today with positive thoughts and expectations.

I overheard my mother talking to my brother in the kitchen, and my brother saying, "I will take him."

My mother said "Okay, take him this weekend."

With that, my brother came out of the kitchen and kind of looked at me with sorrow before heading to his room.

I walked into the kitchen where my mother was sitting at the table, and she had a sad look on her face but quickly tried to hide it and said, "Come here."

I walked over, and she just hugged me for a long time without letting go. I knew something was up, but I didn't know what. That weekend my mother came into my room at the crack of dawn and told me to get up and get dressed. She began packing a bag, going through my closet and dresser drawers, asking me, "Do you want this shirt, or these pants?" After packing a bag, she informed me that I was going to stay with my sister in Chicago for a little while. I found this odd, but I didn't question it too much because it meant getting away from Streamwood for a little while. I headed downstairs and out of the house to find my brother standing by the car waiting for my mother and I. After driving us to the train station, as my brother and I were about to get on the train, my mother gave my brother some last-minute instructions. She then turned her attention to me.

My mother didn't cry much and was very strong, so I knew something was going on when she teared up. My mother was very loving, but she didn't show a lot of weakness. For example, one time my brother called collect, and I answered the phone. When I accepted the charges and asked where he was, he said he was in jail. I freaked out, screaming for my mother, who came to the phone.

She got on the phone and after listening for a minute, calmly said, "I told you if you ever wound up in jail, I was not coming to get you!" and hung the phone up. I knew from all the cop shows I watched that you only got one phone call.

When I told my mother this, she calmly said, "I know, and I will tell you the same thing I told him; if you wind up in jail, I am NOT coming to get you!" I knew she was worried, but she did not show it.

My mother was also a no-nonsense woman who demanded respect and kind of scared me at times. One morning my brother argued with my mother and told her he wasn't going to school that day. She calmly said, "Oh, you are going to school today."

He raised his voice at her, saying, "No, I am not."

All I saw was my brother flying out of the kitchen, jumping down the stairs, opening the front door and rushing through it. As the door slammed shut, the cast iron skillet with MY breakfast in it hit the door where my brother's head would have been.

My mother saw me and looked me in the eye and calmly asked, "Am I going to have a problem with you going to school today?"

I quickly replied, "No ma'am, I was just leaving." I grabbed my book bag and ran out of the door.

In all my 12 years I had never seen my mother cry. To see these tears streaming down her face as I stood there with my bags in my hands alarmed me, puzzled me, and made me sad as well. So as you can imagine, to see this strong woman begin to cry not only made me sad but kind of freaked me out. My mother let me out of her bear hug and said, "Call me when you get to your sister's house."

On the metro train, I kept asking my brother questions, but like my mother, he seemed sad and just kept saying, "You will see, just sit back." My brother was also being nice to me, which made me even more inquisitive and nervous. After a while, my brother tapped me and said,

"Look." Through the window, I saw these huge buildings that took my breath away because they reached all the way up to the sky!

I had only been downtown once before, when I was a really young kid. My mother held my hand when I saw this man that looked so sad. He was in a wheelchair, and he didn't have any legs. I snatched away from my mother and ran to this man, jumping in his lap telling him, "Smile, it's going to be okay." My mother caught up with me, pulling me away from the man and apologizing to him.

The man had the biggest smile on his face and was chuckling. "It's okay, ma'am." He looked at me and said, "Thank you, that's the first time I have smiled in a long time, but you have to be a good boy and listen to your mother, okay?"

I said, "Okay."

After we walked away, my mother scolded me. "Don't ever snatch away from me again. Understand?" I shook my head yes and began questioning my mother about the man. That's when I found out he was homeless, and I knew I wanted to help people like him when I grew up.

Seeing the tall building on my way to my sister's house in Chicago made me remember the walks I took downtown with my mother. My brother and I were now off the train and were now on a bus headed to my sister's house. We were now walking down the street to my sister's house, and my brother, who was playing with me since we got off the train, started giving me advice. He told me to always be aware of my surroundings, and if something didn't feel right—run. He reminded me of things he showed me when he taught me how to fight.

We finally arrived at my sister's house; my brother got a key that was hidden on the front porch, and we went in. My sister's house was nothing like the house in Streamwood, but it was nice.

The house was connected to a house just like it on either side, and it had three levels. Upstairs is where the three bedrooms were, the main level had a living room and dining room, and then there was a full unfinished basement where the washing machine and dryer were. My brother and I hung out with a couple of his friends that he knew somehow in the neighborhood. One of them lived a few blocks away from my sister's house. His name was Duke, and he looked like a giant! Duke was about 6'7", light complected with huge hands and a big Afro.

"What's up, little man," he said with his big voice.

My brother looked at me and said, "If you have any problems, you go to Duke and he will take care of it."

"That's right, little man," said Duke. "If you need anything, I got you, bro!"

My sister showed up, and you could tell she just got home from work. I ran up to her and gave her a hug. My sister was like a second mother even though I didn't see her that often when I lived in Streamwood. My sister stood about 5'5" which was a little taller than my mother; she had a light complexion and long flowing black hair. My sister had a husband named McKinley; he was highly intelligent. He was brown complected, with glasses and an Afro. When he spoke, he would use these big words that I didn't always understand.

I had two nieces; the baby was Michelle and my other niece, who was 7 years younger than me, was Nicole. I was 12 going on 13 years old, and Nicole was 5 going on 6 years old. My sister laid out the chores and duties around the house, and that is when she informed me that I would be baby-sitting Nicole. When I spoke to my mother that evening, I found out I would be living with my sister and going to school from her house until she could get a place for us to live in Chicago. It was another blow. I found myself once again in an environment that I didn't know and in a situation where I didn't know what to expect. I was angry all over again.

CHAPTER EIGHT

THE BUTTERFLY EFFECT

"You Talk Funny." Different city, different kids, same issues.

I was enrolled in a Catholic school right across the street from my sister's house. I now had to wear a red and gray uniform to school every day. On my first day, my niece Nicole and I walked across the street to the school. It wasn't as big as the boarding school, but it was a decent size with a lot of kids. There was a big church in the front of the school, attached to a long older building with a lot of windows. As we walked up, there were two sets of double doors, with a large group of kids in front of each.

Nicole whispered to me, "You go in through there with the big kids." I was in seventh grade, and I assumed that this door was for seventh and eighth grade. I walked up and just kind of stood in the back. The kids begin to stare, point, and giggle as I tried my best to blend into the background. It felt like déjà vu, the only difference being these kids were not white, they looked like me. I felt aggravated because, once again, I was confused. I didn't understand why I was being singled out, because we looked alike.

One of the kids walked up and asked me, "You new here?"

I said, "Yeah."

He then asked, "Where are you from?"

I said, "Streamwood."

From that one-word answer he and others start to laugh. He looked at me with a weird look on his face and said, "Streamwood?" in a voice like he was white. He added, "Cool, that's awesome. Where is that at?"

I knew at that point to keep my mouth shut. This kid was taller and bigger than me, and honestly, I didn't know if I could take him. I also had to take into account that he had a group of friends that seem to be his crew.

The bell rang and we went inside, as we got into the hallway, I could still hear this boy mocking me as he and his crew walked behind me. I overheard a group of girls speaking about how there were two seventh grade home rooms, and they were both upstairs. I followed them up the stairs to the hallway where the two seventh grade classrooms were. I was in Ms. Pruitt's classroom. Instead of asking anyone, trying to keep a low profile, I read the names on the doors until I found her classroom. Upon entering, I went up to her and introduced myself, thinking that the seats were assigned.

She looked at me and said, "Hello, put your coat and bookbag in the closet behind me, then grab a desk and sit down."

After hanging up my coat and putting up my book bag, I grabbed a desk. I noticed that the kid that was mocking me and his crew were in my class. I remember thinking, *Just great!*

As class began, I began thinking, *Okay, if I can just stay quiet and to myself* … and then I heard, "Okay, Class, we have a new student." I yelled in my head, *DAMN!*

She went on to have me stand as she told the class my name was Phillip. She then asked what school I had transferred from.

I replied, "Glenbrook."

"Glenbrook? I never heard of that school. Where is that?"

I said, as the kids were already snickering and whispering, "It's in Streamwood."

She looked at me with a smirk and blurted out, "You are making that up; there is no place called Streamwood. Sit down!"

I sat back down feeling like, *Why? Why do I have to go through this? What did I do to deserve this?*

Lunch time finally rolled around, and as we made our way out of the classroom, a group of girls walked up to me. "So where did you say you are from?"

I repeated myself with the one word answer I gave earlier and said, "Streamwood."

One girl said, "You talk funny," while another girl said, "Why do you sound all proper?" and yet another girl added, "Yeah, like a white boy."

A fourth asked me, "Were there a lot of white people where you were?"

I muttered, "Yeah," as the girls walked away saying, "See you later, white boy."

As I kept walking by myself, I literally bumped into this guy who said, "Hey, what's up?"

I said, "Hi."

Then he said, "My name is Gavin, what is yours?"

I said, "My name is Phillip."

Without questioning me about where I was from, or making fun of me or the way I spoke he asked, "Do you want to be friends?"

I said, "Sure."

To which he replied, "Okay, we are friends." He was in the other seventh grade classroom down the hall. Little did I know that I didn't just make a friend, but someone who I would call my brother.

As we walked our separate ways, I saw and heard a lot of the boys and girls saying, "Yo, Gavin, what's up," and clapping hands with him. There were a lot of girls that drew his name out on their notebooks and giggled and waved as he waved back. I ate lunch by myself, which I was happy to do. But when it was time to make our way back to the classroom, I had just about the whole class laughing at me and taunting me in the hallway. When we got into the classroom, Ms. Pruitt tried to calm everyone down, but the noise didn't totally stop. She tried to teach again but there were still bursts of jokes.

Ms. Pruitt got annoyed and asked, "What is so funny?"

Frank which was the big kid I met with his crew earlier, in his best white voice impersonation, said, "Gee, gosh, nothing, Ms. Pruitt."

Ms. Pruitt smiled, then said, "Cut it out and leave that boy alone!"

After school, I rushed out as fast as I could to get my niece and get away from this place. I managed to find her as she was standing outside and ready to go, I rushed up to her and grabbed her hand and started walking so fast that she could barely keep up. We only got a few steps away from the school before you could hear kids yelling all kinds of white impressions at me. We got home, and I plopped down on the couch, holding my head and covering my face.

Nicole said, "Don't let them bother you."

"You don't understand," I said. "It's not that easy."

She shrugged her shoulders and started fixing herself a peanut butter and jelly sandwich.

I was sitting there pondering how to handle this new predicament when the doorbell rang. I got up to see who was at the door, and it was Gavin. I opened the door, and he said, "Hey, what's up? Can you come out?"

I said, "No, I have to watch my niece, and I can't have company."

He said, "Well, can you come out on the porch and talk?" I didn't see the harm in that, so I left the door open, put on my coat and stood on the porch. We talked for a little bit and then he asked, "Man, where are you from?"

Expecting the ridicule, I said, "Streamwood."

And he said, "Ah, that's cool."

I told him that I needed to get back in the house and watch my niece, make sure she did her homework, do my chores, and do my homework too. He asked if I could hang out for a little bit when my sister got home. I told him I would ask. When my sister got home, and she was satisfied that everything was done, she asked about my day, to which I replied, "I don't want to talk about it."

She said, "Oh, it wasn't good, huh? It will get better."

Just then the doorbell rang again, and it was Gavin. My sister asked, "Who is this?"

I said, "Oh, we go to school together, can I go outside?"

She said, "On a school night, I think not."

I said, "Well, can I just go in the front?"

She agreed, and I walked outside. Gavin had a football, so we played catch for a little while before sitting on the porch to talk.

As we were talking, I kept using phrases like "excellent" and "that's awesome." Gavin laughed and said, "Okay, we are going to have to change the way you talk; you are going to have to learn how to blend in."

He went on to say, "Instead of excellent, say that's dope, and instead of that's awesome say that's cool." He said not to worry about it because he would teach me.

My sister came to the door and said it was time to come in. I introduced her to Gavin and then told him that I would see him at school the next day. When I got in the house, McKinley, my brother-in-law was home. I don't know if I was misreading his mood or not, but he didn't seem too enthused to have me there. My sister was serving dinner and asked again about my day. I remained silent. My brother-in-law spoke up and said, "Boy, didn't you hear her talking to you? Answer her!" He had this stare like I better get to talking or he was going to hurt me.

Before I had a chance to speak, my sister said, "That's okay, I know this transition is hard but try to make the best of it."

My brother-in-law, who was still staring at me, said, "Boy, the next time someone asks you a question, you better answer, do you understand?"

I said, "Yes." At that point it was time to get ready for bed. We had to shower or take a bath, put our pj's on and get in the bed.

I asked myself, *What is this? I am not a kid!* First of all, I showered in the morning before school; second, I had a much later bedtime, and I governed myself. Last, but not least, I was very unhappy at the fact I had to share a bedroom with my nieces. I began to protest but was quickly shut down; it was two against one.

The next day didn't get any better. It was like everyone went home and watched reruns of *Leave it to Beaver* so they could come back to school to have new ways to make fun of me or insult me. This eventually did die down, but it never died out. About midyear it had gotten to the point that even the kids that were outcasts themselves were trying to use me to get in with the other kids. There was this one kid that, during a bathroom break, decided to kick the stall door open while I was peeing. He and the other kids laughed so hard and thought that it was so funny they couldn't contain themselves. By this time, I had so much anger, frustration, and negativity built up in me that I began keeping mental tallies so that I could take revenge.

I waited for this kid to enter a stall and take a crap, and just as he got into his grunt, I acted! I kicked the door in with all of my might with a bathroom filled with kids so I could embarrass the hell out of him, since it was taboo to take a dump in school. But as usual, life just didn't like me. Instead of laughter and everything that this kid received when he did it to me, everyone started yelling that I was trying to see his privates. It got so loud Ms. Pruitt busted into the bathroom screaming, "What is going on

here?"

The kid, who had gotten his pants up but was still in the stall,

yelled, "He kicked the door in trying to see my thing."

Ms. Pruitt looked at me in disgust in front of all of the other kids in

the bathroom and said, "What are you? Some kind of pervert?" And then

she yelled, "ARE YOU A …?" Well, let's just say that on that day, she

used a derogatory word for a homosexual!

I was pissed and tried to explain to her. "No, he kicked in the door

on me the other day when I was trying to—"

But before I could finish my sentence, she said, "You are nasty;

wash your hands and come out of here."

My blood was boiling, and all I could see was red. I had a new

target now; the other kid could wait. I knew what kind of car Ms. Pruitt

drove, so I enlisted Gavin to stay after school with me. I gave Nicole the

house key and sent her home. I waited for the crowds of kids to leave the

school, and once I felt the coast was clear, I had Gavin lead me to the

teachers' parking lot. Once we got there, I confirmed with Gavin the car that Ms. Pruitt drove. I told Gavin, "Look out and tell me if someone is coming."

Gavin asked, "Man, what are you doing?"

"Just look out and tell me if someone is coming!" I replied. I made my way over to Ms. Pruitt's car and removed the air cap from each tire to let the air out until they were all completely flat. When I was done, I put the air cap back on each one. After we left, Gavin couldn't believe what I had just done.

I explained why I did it, and he said, "Yeah, I heard about that."

The next morning, I was called into the principal's office as soon as I walked in the door. The principal was a short, heavy woman who was a nun. She was dark complected and wore glasses. When I got to the principal's office, Ms. Pruitt was there, in tears and crying. The principal asked me to shut the door and proceeded to tell me that I was seen around Ms. Pruitt's car the day prior and that all four of her tires were flat. I gave a devious grin and said, "Yeah, I let the air out of all of her tires."

The principal and Ms. Pruitt sat stunned, staring at me.

After a few minutes, Ms. Pruitt got upset and started to explain that I was a problem in her classroom.

The principal asked me, "Why would you do that?"

I responded in a raised voice, "Because she called me a f@#ot!"

The principal angrily asked, "And why would she do that?"

I finally had the chance to explain how I was being picked on daily, how this kid kicked in the door while I was trying to pee, and how he and all the other kids laughed. "I decided to retaliate by kicking in the door on him to show him how it felt, and Ms. Pruitt wouldn't even listen to my side of the story!"

The principal sat with an amazed look before saying, "Okay, Phillip, thank you, go back to class."

When I opened the office door, Gavin was sitting outside. I looked back at the principal and said, "Gavin didn't have anything to do with this; I did this by myself."

The principal called Gavin in and asked, "Is this true?"

And he said, "Yeah."

The principal said, "Okay, go to class." I don't think Gavin has forgiven me to this day for that incident. His mother was just as strict as mine and he avoided trouble like the plague.

Ms. Pruitt showed up in class a half an hour later and was very subdued and quiet. She began to tiptoe around me, and you could tell that she didn't really want to deal with me. I felt bad, especially after I heard about all she had to go through just to get home that day, as well as having to have each tire looked at to be sure it didn't have a hole. But I still felt vindicated, saying to myself, *I bet you she won't call me that again.*

The bullying from the kids in the school eased up, but it never stopped, and one day when I came to class, a group of kids were saying that this kid was saying stuff about me. One of the things was that he would have kicked my butt. I immediately confronted this kid and got in his face, challenging him to do something. He began explaining that he didn't say it and that it was Gavin that said it. It just so happened that Gavin was walking past the door on the way to his classroom. I jumped in front of him and said, "You are talking crap about me?" and then punched him in the chest, knocking him into the group of kids that had started to form. He jumped up in anger, but before he could swing back, the teachers broke us up.

After coming back to class from the principal's office, one of the girls said it was the kid that I confronted that was the one talking mess. She said Gavin never said anything, and then she shook her head and called me stupid. I caught the kid I had confronted alone and told him that if he talked stuff about me again, I would kick his butt. With a scared look on his face, he again tried to blame Gavin, but I said, "I know it was you, and you heard what I said."

I found Gavin at the end of the day and apologized to him, explaining what actually happened. He said, "It's cool, but you know we have to finish this." I guess for his own ego he wanted to finish the fight that I started. By this time, we were pretty close, and I was beginning to understand him more and more. So I agreed to finish the fight.

I knew all of his sisters and had met his mother. He had three sisters. One went to the same school as us. She was about 5'3", light complected with shoulder-length hair, and she wore glasses. She was very quiet and soft spoken. You usually had to ask her to repeat herself because she spoke so softly. He had another sister that was very athletic and tough. She was about 5'6" with an athletic build. She was light complected with short hair, and she wore glasses.

There was one time when Gavin challenged her to a foot race and asked me to join in because I was pretty fast. Without skipping a beat, she kicked off her shoes and said, "I will beat you all barefoot!" You have to remember we were talking about the street on the South Side of Chicago where there was plenty of broken glass and garbage. We raced, and she beat us. I was amazed at her determination and speed with no shoes on her feet. Towards the end of the race, it was down to me and her and all she kept saying was: "Come on, come on, you think you got me beat? Come on!" I was giving it all I had, and she was right there with me, beating me easily in the end. Then there was his oldest sister, who was dark complected and heavyset. She had medium-length curly hair, and she also wore glasses. She loved to play around a lot and would antagonize Gavin.

We walked to Gavin's house, which was a large older house with a fenced-in yard. We stepped inside of the fence.

Gavin looked at me and said, "Well, are you ready?"

I sat my bag down and said, "Okay, come on."

We kept circling each other, so I started to chuckle a little. Gavin seemed to have gotten annoyed and said, "Oh, this isn't a joke," and swung at me. He landed a punch on my shoulder, and it hurt, which told me he was serious. I didn't really want to fight, so I wouldn't swing back. He threw a couple more punches that hurt, which then caused me to start swinging back. I knew from the grunts he made when a punch landed that I hurt him as well. All in all, we called the fight, Gavin was getting the best licks in because I didn't really want to fight, and his younger sister ran in the house yelling, "They are fighting!" By the time she was able to get Gavin's mother outside, the fight was over. Gavin landed the most punches, including the one he landed on my chest toward the end of the fight, I guess this made us even in Gavin's eyes.

After the fight, we picked up where we had left off, like nothing happened. You would think things would have calmed down at school, but instead it was like the kids wanted blood. They wouldn't let up and tried their best to instigate a fight between Gavin and me. When they couldn't rattle Gavin and get him to fight me, they came after me, relentlessly trying to get me to go back after him. One day when I came to school, the pressure got to be too much. It was that day that I learned a lesson about human nature, but one that to this day doesn't make any sense to me. Before school, I guess the kids realized that they weren't going to get another fight out of Gavin and me, so I guess they wanted some kind of reaction out of me to satisfy their blood lust.

That day, they came at me in every way imaginable, from talking about my mother to whatever they could find about me or my personality. As I walked into the classroom, I was already at boiling point but quiet. The kids kept on with the taunting and laughing as quietly as they could but soon it got loud with laughter. Ms. Pruitt asked, "What is so funny?" When she didn't immediately get an answer, she called on Frank.

"What is so funny? I want to laugh too!" she said in a sarcastic voice. I don't remember the joke; I just remember her reaction to it when Frank told her. She looked at me and began to snicker, trying to hold her laughter in. While choking back the laughter, she said, "Leave that boy alone."

Do you remember what I said about the lesson I learned that day about human nature? I stood up, pushing my desk out of the way, and yelled, "No, keep it going because it is so f*@ing funny! I am the biggest joke in this f*@#ing school, right?!" The thing I didn't and don't understand is how people can push you to the edge of insanity, and then look at you with a shocked look on their face when you snap! They look at you like you are the one that is crazy, and like they are totally innocent and had nothing to do with why you are going off. As I walked toward the door of the classroom, I glanced over at Ms. Pruitt, and she had this look of shame on her face. I turned around at the doorway, stuck both my middle fingers up, and screamed, "F all of you!"

As I was turning back around, I saw two female students stand up and ask Ms. Pruitt if they could go after me. I heard her say, "No, let him go." I walked all the way out of the school and outside before I realized that it was in the middle of winter in Chicago. I also quickly realized that the keys to the house were in my coat pocket in the classroom I had just stormed out of. I hadn't even got halfway down the block that day, before I found out what the Windy City Hawk was that I had heard so much about.

Chicago's wind is often called "The Hawk", and the Hawk said to me,
"You can't get in the house without your keys, are you sure you want to
stay out here with me? Or do you want to swallow your pride and take
your butt back into that school?"

I dropped my head and turned around because it was freezing, and
that hawk was no joke. When I made it back into the school, I dreaded
going back into the classroom I had just made a huge scene in. When I
finally walked back in, you could hear a pin drop. The two female students
that wanted to come after me looked at me with empathy as I sat back
down in my seat. Later that day on the way to lunch, the two female
students caught me in the hallway and pulled me to the side. They both
asked, "Are you okay?"

I said, "Yeah, I am just tired of the crap."

One of the girls said, "Don't take that crap, give it back!"

The other girl agreed and said, "Yeah, you shut everyone up when
you snapped earlier, and I don't blame you."

They left me with a smile on my face because they both blushed
and told me that they thought that I was kind of cute before giggling as

they walked away. Things toned down as the rest of the school year began to wind down and head into summer. Word started getting around about what happened that day, and the kids started saying that I was crazy. Like I said earlier, I don't get how you play with the bull and then call the bull crazy when he gives you the horns.

Summer finally rolled around, and I was so happy to see it come. I admired Gavin. He introduced me to a lot of fun things, like inner city football, which was different from playing football in Streamwood. In city football you played on the city streets with all kinds of trash. There was an instance where Gavin was thrown a pass that went over his head. He dove for it and caught it with one hand and came down on his right hand, which landed on a broken bottle that cut his palm wide open. He called time out, and as he picked the glass out of his hand, ran into the house. He came back out with his hand wrapped and said, "Okay, that was a touchdown, 14 to 7 our way."

We played between parked cars and traffic. In Streamwood we had open fields to play football in. Also, in city football you used car bumpers to mark the touchdown area, and you had makeshift rules. You had to make your own calls, which got interesting at times. A fight could easily break out over a call that someone didn't agree with, and usually the one with the biggest voice or who refused to back down would win the call.

I was also introduced to street basketball, which was played in an alley with a crate that the bottom was cut out of. Street basketball had the same premise of calling your own calls and makeshift rules that could usually lead to the game going on and on because of all of the arguing over calls and fouls. I was also introduced to my first Chicago crush. I was walking home one day after playing basketball and caught a glimpse of this beautiful girl in the window of her apartment which was right next door to me.

She was dark complected with long hair past her shoulders and a petite frame. She had large breasts, and a nice plump round butt. She was wearing the same school uniform that we wore every day. Her skirt was shorter than the rest of the girls, which showed off her muscular legs. I waved, and she smiled and waved back. I took a few more steps before turning around and going back. She was still in the window, struggling to open it, when I went back. She saw me and smiled again as she finally got the window opened. She said, "Whew, it's hot in here." After a quick pause she said, "Hi."

I said, "Hi, what's your name?"

She said, "Tamara. What's yours?" After I told her, she asked, "Don't you live next door?"

I shyly said, "Yeah." I asked if she went to the school I went to, and she answered yes.

I asked, "Why are you wearing your uniform in the summer?"

In a playful banter, she quickly answered, "Because I like the way it makes my booty look," as she provocatively turned sideways and posed.

As my eyes popped out of my head, she added, "I am just kidding. I have to go to summer school." I asked how old she was, and she asked me, "How old do I look?"

I said, "Um, I don't know."

I asked her if she could come outside, and she explained that she had a strict mother and that she couldn't, but she could talk to me through the window. I needed to get home myself in order to meet the time I was told to be home, so I asked if I could call her, and of course for the same reason, the answer was no. I asked if I could see her, and she answered with a smile. "Maybe." I told her I had to go, and she told me she would see me around. For a few days, I would meet her at her window, and we would talk and flirt back and forth. One day I caught her outside on her way into her apartment. We talked and flirted, but it was rushed because she had to call her mother by a certain time, or she would be in trouble. That day before she rushed into her apartment, she asked me if she could give me a hug, and of course I said yes. She hugged me and then kissed me on the cheek before giggling and running off. I was on Cloud Nine-and-a-half!

After that I pretty much stalked her apartment window, trying to just catch a glimpse of her. To no avail. It was like she disappeared. I went back to hanging out with Gavin but kept Tamara in the back of my mind. One evening while hanging out in a local game room, I was introduced to something that was the complete opposite of what my summer experience had been up to that point. Gavin and I took turns on Gallagher which was a popular video game in the '80s. It was Gavin's turn, and as I hovered over his back watching him play, about eight to ten guys walked in, crowding the game room. This made me extremely uncomfortable, and I whispered to Gavin, "Let's go, I don't like this." Without even turning around, Gavin told me to hold on because he wanted to finish his game.

I said, "You stay and finish if you want to; I will be outside."

As I turned around to leave Gavin said, "Hold on, I am almost done."

I began to walk into the crowd when I heard, "That's the one that's been talking to your woman." What seemed to be the leader looked past me and yelled, "What's up, Gavin?"

Gavin picked up his head just quick enough to see who it was and yelled back, "What up, Anthony?"

I began to squeeze past the crowd, hoping just to slip out unnoticed, but Anthony stood in my way. As I pushed past him, I said in a low voice, "Excuse me."

Anthony replied, "What did you say about my mama?"

Annoyed, I turned around and looked at him and scoffed. When I turned back to continue my exit, Anthony punched me in the back of my head. I spun around, grabbed him by the front of his shirt collar, and drew my fist back. It felt like the room stood up and quickly closed in on me, begging me to hit him. I slowly let him go, saying I didn't want any problems. I made it outside, but as I went out the door, I heard what sounded like an army following me. I continued to walk slowly to the alley, but once I made it to the opening of the alleyway, I took off like my feet were on fire. The alley was made of gravel, and I was running so hard that I was kicking up gravel and dust. I glanced behind me. Leading the pack was Anthony, who fell to the wayside because he was winded, but not before grabbing a bottle off of the ground and throwing it at me.

I was running so fast that the bottle didn't even come close. I made it to my sister's backyard where I found a spot to hide until I could be sure no one was still chasing me. After a little while, I heard Gavin come to my sister's house looking for me. He told my sister that some older kids were chasing me, and he didn't know where I went. I waited for him to leave, angry at the fact that he hadn't left the game room when I wanted to and wondering why he didn't have my back. I also didn't want him to see that I had been crying because I didn't understand why I seemed to attract trouble and negativity. I didn't fit in with the white kids because of my skin color, and I didn't fit in with my own kind because of the way I spoke or carried myself. I avoided going outside for a few days after that until one day Gavin came by. He asked me what happened, and I explained it to him, to which he replied that he didn't see or hear anything.

He went on to tell me about how Anthony was in a gang—I didn't even know what that was—but that he was harmless. I didn't know what to make of it, was Gavin wanting to pretend like he didn't know what was going on? I decided to let it go because Gavin had been such a good friend. I put my paranoia away and believed him. One day I walked past Tamara's apartment building, and she was tapping frantically on the window. I stopped to talk to her, but she never opened the window. Instead, she turned some slow music on and began to dance provocatively in the window. I couldn't believe what I was seeing. She opened her shirt a little and showed her white lace bra and rubbed her butt. She then lifted her school skirt up and showed her white lace panties. I stood there in amazement as she put her finger up to gesture for me to wait a minute and disappeared from the window.

After a minute, she opened the curtains to reveal her standing in nothing but her panties and bra. My mouth dropped open and before I could utter a word, Anthony appeared in the window in nothing but his underwear! I was so angry, frustrated, and aggravated as they stood in the window pointing at me and laughing hysterically. I picked up a rock and hurled it at the window. Anthony yelled, "Mother f!%@#r," as he started grabbing his clothes like he was going to come outside. Instead of running away, I guess like they expected me to, I stood there. She opened the window and told me not to speak to her or come around her building anymore. I remember thinking, *I live right next door!* I stood there silent, and after a minute she said to Anthony, "Come on, let's do it."

Anthony said, "What about him?"

She said, "Let him stand there and watch."

As she took off her bra, Anthony looked at me and laughed as he pulled the curtain shut. As I walked off, I thought about the incident in the game room and remembered hearing one of the guys say, "That's the dude that be talking to your woman right there." I later found out that Tamara was a problem child that got a lot of attention from bad boys. I heard that she popped up pregnant, unsure of who the father was.

Summer came to a bittersweet end, and it was time for school again. As much as I did not want to go back to the place that I deemed hell, I got some uplifting news that made it a pill I could swallow. My mother was close to closing on a condo, and I would be moving back in with her soon. I began the school year with my eighth-grade teacher, Mrs. Harris. The school mixed the homeroom classrooms from the year before, which put new students that I hadn't known in the classroom.

I don't know if I was just starting to notice girls more or if it was the fact that there were just some beautiful girls in our classroom. One of these girls had me mesmerized. She was dark complected, short, with a beautiful smile and an athletic body. The thing about her was she was very sophisticated and carried herself differently from the other girls. I admired her from afar, not wanting to get shot down like an unsuspecting deer during hunting season, especially knowing I wasn't the most popular guy in school. This year was a little different in the fact that the kids still went after me but not as hard as they did in the previous year, with the exception of this one kid named Keith, who seemed to be the school bully.

Keith was short, dark complected with a stocky football build. He would crack jokes about me and pick at me, but I stayed silent and ignored him. One day Mrs. Harris left the classroom, and Keith started his antics. I ignored him and continued my schoolwork. He cracked a joke, which instead of being quiet about, I responded to. I quickly cracked a joke about him which got a bigger laugh than what he'd got from his joke about me. He grabbed a bucket of water that was used to clean the chalkboard. He said, "Dare me that I won't pour this on you."

I said in a calm voice, "Don't do it, Keith."

The girl I admired yelled at Keith. "Would you grow up and go sit down!"

He said it again. "Dare me."

I went to reply, but before I could say anything, he poured the whole bucket of water on me and then tried to hit me with the bucket. I quickly stood up in disbelief, wet where he'd poured the dirty water all in my lap. I walked toward Keith, who started backing up toward the blackboard. I distracted him by saying, "Oh hey, Mrs. Harris." When he looked, I grabbed him by the back of his head and pushed him face first as hard as I could into the blackboard. When I let his head go, he turned and looked at me with a disoriented look as his nose began to bleed heavily. As I walked back to my seat, I caught the eye of the girl I admired from afar only to see a displeased look on her face. She said, "I expected more of you, Phillip."

That made me feel bad, because if this girl had said jump, I would have asked her, "How high?" But then I got upset because what was I supposed to do? I was so confused and disappointed in myself at the same time. There were a few kids in our classroom that were classified as "thuggish" or "bad boys." To this day, I still don't get why women go for this type versus the guy like myself who is the opposite of that. Things got worse after that day between Keith and I, as he recruited more and more kids to taunt and torment me. Keith took it to a whole different level by playing mind games with me. One time he showed up at my house claiming he wanted to be friends. Gavin showed up with a puzzled look shortly after. He asked me, "What's he doing here?"

With my own puzzled look, I said, "He said he wants to be friends."

Keith said, "Yeah, let's all be friends," as he pushed past me and into my house. It was a very strict rule that I couldn't have company when my sister wasn't at home. Before I could say anything, Gavin said, "I thought you couldn't have company?"

"I can't!" I said.

Gavin followed me into the house and said, "Hey, Keith, man, you got to go."

Keith sat down on the couch and said, "I ain't going nowhere."

At that point I heard keys, and I said, "Oh man, my sister came home from work early. Hide!"

Gavin hid behind the front door, while Keith said, "I ain't hiding!"

As I stepped toward Keith, as the door swung open. My sister looked over at the couch where he was sitting, smiling, and then looked at me and said, "Your ass is grass, and I am the lawnmower!" She went to shut the door and saw Gavin. She said, "Hello Gavin."

Gavin nervously replied, "Hello, may I leave?"

"Yes, you may." She then looked at Keith and said, "I think you should leave too."

As Keith left, laughing loudly, I told him how much I hated him.

Another incident took place that was bound to happen as tension, anger, and frustration built up between Keith and I which made for a bad outcome for him in the end. One day Keith started in with his normal mind games and daily antics. He was on point that day, getting laughs at my expense and seriously getting under my skin. We had a test that day and the room was silent as everyone worked busily on their tests. I was trying my best to calm down and concentrate on my work, when Keith, who sat in front of me, began whispering and taunting me. I hadn't said a word when Mrs. Harris called on me to be quiet. I tried to tell her that it was Keith not me, but she said, "I don't want to hear it, be quiet or I am calling your mother!"

Shortly afterwards, Keith started taunting me again. Mrs. Harris said, "I said be quiet. That's it, I am calling your mother."

When she left the room to go and call my mother, Keith turned completely around in his seat and taunted me even louder.

I said in a low voice, "Stop f@*king with me, Keith."

He said, "Awe, poor baby got in trouble with his mommy? Awe."

I said in a louder voice, "Stop f@*king with me, Keith."

Mrs. Harris came back into the room, and he was still taunting me in a whisper.

Mrs. Harris yelled at me. "I have already called your mother. Do you need me to call her back?"

After a few minutes, Keith whispered, "You are pathetic," and laughed quietly.

I stood up and yelled, "I told you to stop f@*king with me Keith!" Then I grabbed my desk, picked it up, and brought it down, hitting him in the back of the head with it. I don't totally remember what happened because I blacked out. What I was told was that I turned Keith over and began punching him in the face. The girl that I admired screamed my name as Mrs. Harris tried pulling me off him. I snapped back to myself when Mrs. Harris told me to go to the principal's office. I looked around the classroom thinking, *what just happened?* On my way out, the girl I admired looked at me and shook her head with discontent, while everyone else looked shocked and in disbelief. It was found out that Keith began the incident by taunting me, and that he had been bullying me since the school year began. He was expelled, while I was made to see a psychiatrist for anger management in order to avoid expulsion.

Towards the end of that school year, my mother was able to close on a condo on 71st and South Shore Drive. It was a three-bedroom condo with a floor plan that went from one side of the building to the other. It had a huge front room that spread out into an attached sunroom. I had to be bussed back and forth since the school was so far away. But at least I had my mother back. One of the things I've learned is you have to be careful who you share your weaknesses with because some people can't wait for the opportunity to use them against you.

CHAPTER NINE

IT TAKES COURAGE TO LOVE

Love starts with a smile, grows with a kiss, and ends

with a tear.

The school year didn't get any better as I was the easy target and the butt of a lot of the jokes. But I did meet my first black girlfriend at school, which was another piece of good news outside of having my mother back. Her name was Keshia. She was very dark, complete with shoulder length hair and an average body. She was average height with an outgoing personality. She was in seventh grade, and I was in eighth. She knew about how I was treated at school and sympathized. I guess she sympathized because she was often made fun of because of her skin tone, but she was popular for the most part because she was very quick-witted with an attitude. It was easy for her to come back at anyone that had something to say about her, backed up with a fiery temper, which made people back down.

By this time, we had moved into a house that my mother was buying on 91st and Harper which was a lot closer to where Keshia lived, but I would not be caught anywhere close to her house. Her father was an ex-NFL football player. He was 7'1" and about 340 lbs—this man was huge. The rule was Keshia could not date, so we had to sneak around, but it always made me nervous hoping that her father wouldn't find out. One day Keshia pressured me into coming over, and I relented. Her bedroom was in the attic. The attic was remodeled for her to give her a private room away from her two sisters. While I was at her house, she kept trying to get me upstairs. I was very reluctant because I would be trapped upstairs if her mother or abnormally humongous father came home. She eventually got me upstairs, where we began kissing and making out. I never took it too far, respecting the fact that Keshia was a virgin.

Well, do you remember earlier when I told you about her outgoing personality? True to her nature, when I wouldn't go beyond a certain point, she attacked me. She began stripping my clothes off, and just as we seriously started getting into it, her younger sister burst in and screamed, "Ooo, Keshia!"

Keshia screamed, "Get out!" She got her little sister out of the room, but by that time I was ready to go.

All I kept thinking about was that her sister was going to tell, and her father was going to rip me in half like a piece of loose-leaf paper. Keshia tried to get me to continue, but it wasn't going to happen, and I left. After that she was insatiable: she wanted to do it anywhere at any time. I went over one time when no one was home, and Keshia wanted to do it in her sister's room. Her sister's bedroom was on the main floor, so Keshia figured if her sister or anyone came home, she could quickly get me out of the backdoor. Usually, taking all of our clothes off was out of the norm, but we felt comfortable enough that we had the house to ourselves. We heard keys and a deep voice yelling Keshia's name. It was Keshia's dad. Keshia had locked a lock on the front door that no one in the house had the key to. I swallowed my heart, and I believe my soul temporarily left my body.

Keshia shoved me into her sister's walk-in closet as she threw on her robe. I made my way to the back of the closet and hid myself behind the clothes that were hanging in front of me.

He asked Keshia why she was in her robe, to which she quickly responded that she was about to get in the shower.

She asked him why he wasn't at work before pausing and saying, "Are you high again? Did you do some coke?"

He told her no and asked her to go get something he needed for work out of the basement. She went downstairs and when she was gone, he headed straight for the bedroom where I was hiding in the closet. I heard him come into the room and pause; I suspect he was looking around. He then came to the closet and began moving the hanging clothes around like he knew I was there. As the clothes swung back and forth, my knees got weak, and I swung with them while literally praying to God that this giant, who was maybe high on coke, would not find me. The things he would do to me would be unspeakable. Keshia came in and interrupted his search of the closet, telling him to get out of the closet that she shared with her sister. She kept asking him, "Don't you have to go to work? Do you want me to tell Mom that you are not at work?"

He said he was on his way to work and left the house. She laughed with relief and said, "Okay, you can come out now."

I came out, wiping the tears from my eyes as she laughed hysterically at me and the situation. I started getting dressed, and she kept trying to stop me. I said, "Are you crazy?" Once I was dressed, she kept saying that I couldn't leave right away because her father could still be close by. I convinced her to let me out the backdoor instead of the front. I hurdled the gate in her backyard, and once in the alley I ran until I was just tired of running. When I was blocks away from Keshia's house, I stopped to rest. I looked up, and across the street from me, Keshia's father was getting onto a bus. I began to laugh and headed back to Keshia's house. When I got there, Keshia, who was still in her robe but wouldn't let me back in, she said her mother and sister were on the way home.

Keshia and I became very close, until she told me a story about how she and her mother went to a party, and all the teenagers were in the basement together. She said one thing led to another, and three of the boys caught her in the bathroom and took turns raping her. I was pissed and urged her to tell her parents. We were on the phone all night. In order to talk to me on the phone, she would pretend like I was one of her female friends named Phyllis. Towards the end of the night, she began to tell me she made it up and that she had slept with the three guys consensually. I did not believe her, but I didn't know what to think. We got off of the phone that night, but I kept insisting that she should tell her parents, still believing that she was raped. One day after Keshia insisted again that it was consensual, I told her that if that was the case, then it was over! She began to cry and was very distraught. I saw her later that day, and I kept asking her which one it was, was it consensual or was she raped. She said it was consensual.

She was standing in front of a garage, and I pushed her to the side, while I swung at the garage door with everything I had, punching the garage and denting it behind her head. I said some pretty mean things to her ending it with "we are done!" Whenever she would call, I would hang up on her. She would come to my house, and I wouldn't answer the door. I received a call from her one evening with her begging me not to hang up on her. When I asked her what she wanted, she said that she just wanted to say goodbye. I asked her where she was going, and she said away.

I said, "Are you moving?"

She said, "In a way."

I started to get annoyed with her and began getting off of the phone with her, and that's when she informed me that she had taken a whole bunch of pills. I didn't believe her at first, seeing how she played a lot of games and would say anything to keep me on the phone; however, she sounded groggy and seemed disoriented. I asked her why she was trying to kill herself. She stated in a slur that she was tired of everything, from being under such strict parents to being under the pressure of doing well in the new honors classes she was put in at school.

She also talked about how she lost her best friend, the one she could confide her deepest thoughts to. Thinking she was talking about her female friend; I asked her what happened between them. She scoffed and said that she was referring to me, even though she had just had an argument with her other friend, too. I asked her what she had taken, as she sounded more and more disoriented, and either she was an excellent actress, or she really took something. At that point, I clicked over and called an ambulance. It was hard because I had to try to remember her address. I knew how to get to her house but couldn't remember her exact address. The emergency operator was able to use Keshia's phone number to verify her address and dispatched an ambulance.

As Keshia started to fade out, I threatened to call her parents and told her that I just called an ambulance for her. I knew she was serious when I failed to get a reaction out of her, after telling her that. She would have lost it if she was in her right mind, because including her parents would have brought down a crap storm on her. Keshia had her own phone line and was up in the attic away from her family by herself. I had the main house number because Keshia had me call her on it once before. It was supposed to be a one-time use, and she made me promise to dispose of the number and never call it again. As Keshia was fading in and out, I clicked over and called the main house number and her mother answered.

I said, "Hello, ma'am, my name is Phillip, and I know you don't know me."

She quickly interrupted and said, "Well, Keshia can't have boy phone calls!"

I said, "Yes ma'am, I know."

She interrupted again and asked, "How do you know Keshia?"

I said, "We go to school together, ma'am, and I am her boyfriend."

She gasped, but before she could interrupt again, I said, "Ma'am, you and her father can kill me later, but Keshia has taken a bunch of pills. I have her on the other line, and she is falling unconscious."

She screamed, "What! Where is she?"

I said, "She is in her room in the attic. I have already called an ambulance, and they are on the way."

Her mother yelled for Keshia's father, and they both made their way upstairs where they found Keshia in a drugged-up state. Her father took the phone out of Keshia's hand, while her mother started to call Keshia's name and keep her alert.

Her father got on the phone and said, "Hello."

I started to hang up, but instead I said, "Hello, sir, my name is Phillip. Is Keshia okay?"

He yelled to Keshia's mother, "Who the hell is Phillip?"

Keshia's mother explained what I told her as he began to get upset, she yelled, "He is the one who told me about Keshia and called an ambulance!"

By that time, I could hear the siren from the ambulance in the background. Her father got back on the phone with me and said, "Thank you."

I asked if he knew which hospital they were taking her to. He asked the paramedic, who by that time was upstairs. The paramedic told him, and he told me. I asked if I could come visit her, and after hesitating, he said, "Yes."

The next day, I called the hospital, and they put me in touch with Keshia's mother. Her mother indicated what Keshia took and said that they had to pump her stomach. I asked her if I could come to visit Keshia, and she said yes, and that Keshia had been asking for me. I told her mother what time I would be there, and she said okay. When I got to the hospital, her family was not there. I slowly entered Keshia's hospital room thinking she was going to be pissed because of all the trouble she was probably in. I walked in and Keshia was so happy to see me. She called me over to her bed, quickly embraced me, and stole a kiss. She repeatedly apologized and thanked me for calling the ambulance and her parents. She explained that the relationship between her and her parents had completely changed, and that things were not bad enough to try to kill herself.

As we were talking, her mother walked in and said, "So you must be Phillip?"

I said, "Yes ma'am."

She said, "Come here, boy."

I nervously walked over, not knowing what to expect, and she opened her arms and hugged me so tight I could barely breathe!

She looked in my eyes with tears in hers and said, "Thank you."

I said, "You are welcome, and I am sorry that we went behind your back."

She said, "Forget about all of that. I am just happy that you were there."

I asked to speak to her out in the hallway, where I told her about the rape incident and told her I wasn't sure if it was true or not. Her mother informed me that Keshia had told her about it, and that the police were called. They interviewed the boys, who admitted to raping her. We walked back into Keshia's room. I felt so bad because of what she had been through, and because I wasn't there for her. If I had been there to talk to her and listen, then maybe she wouldn't have tried to take her life. Shortly after that, her father came in, and I had that feeling of a worm looking at a bird just before the bird gobbles the worm up.

Keshia's mother said, "This is Phillip."

He stared at me for a moment then stuck his hand out and said, "Hello."

I stuck my hand out too, and his swallowed mine. Then all of a sudden, I felt pain in my hand because he was crushing it. The handshake lasted longer than usual as the pain increased. He let my hand go and said, "Thank you, you can leave now."

I was heading for the door when Keshia's mother told him to stop it and invited me to stay.

He walked over to Keshia and explained to me that this was his baby girl, and he was very protective of her. He then said that he appreciated what I'd done, but it would take a minute to get used to Keshia having a boyfriend.

Keshia and I looked at each other, and then Keshia asked, "So I can have a boyfriend now?"

They said that she and I could see each other under strict supervision.

A little while later, they left to take Keshia's baby sister home. Keshia and I were finally alone. She said, "I want you, let's go in the bathroom!"

I said, "No, you need to stay in the bed."

Keshia became very aggressive; I had never seen her act like this before. She all but dragged me into the bathroom where she quickly locked the door.

A nurse came into the room as we were coming out of the bathroom. She asked, "Were you all just in the bathroom?"

Keshia quickly spoke up and said I was in the bathroom helping her with something. The nurse quickly threatened to kick me out if I acted inappropriately again. After the nurse left, I expressed my concerns.

Keshia told me to shut up and stop acting like I didn't want to mess around in the bathroom too. I had mixed emotions about it because we were in the hospital after she had just tried to take her own life. And on top of that, she had been raped by three guys. I felt low even though Keshia had initiated it. Keshia's personality really changed, and she was not the reserved low-key person I first met. I mean, she was still in there somewhere, but she had been taken over by this new loud, boisterous, and flamboyant person. Keshia and I continued seeing each other until my freshman year of high school. We eventually grew apart.

CHAPTER TEN

URBAN LIVING

The school of hard knocks,

For my freshman year of high school, I went to Hales Franciscan on the South Side of Chicago, which was an all-boys school. There were so many other schools I wanted to go to, but my mother wanted me to concentrate on academics, so she picked Hales because as she said it, "no girls, no distractions." I had some awesome teachers at Hales and I learned a lot. One of those teachers was my English teacher. She introduced me to Maya Angelou, and we had to read *I Know Why the Caged Bird Sings*. Another teacher was my pre-algebra teacher, Father Author. He was so cool and laid back. I was the typical goofy teenager and would do things like slide across the floor in my dress shoes. I would run and slide along the floor of Father Author's classroom every morning. One morning, he said, "Mr. Hanks, if you slide across my classroom floor again, you can slide down to the principal's office."

There were a couple of problems with this school, one being the obvious: no girls! The other problem was that it was dangerous because of the area that the school was located in. Gavin went to this school called St. Willibrord catholic high school that was co-ed and asked me to come too. I asked my mother if I could transfer. It didn't take much to convince her; I'd had a classmate who was on the track team and made all American. His mother threw him a party for his achievement, but I chose not to go. The next morning, he was found in his bathroom, dead. He had smoked a laced joint which caused him to have a heart attack.

But the straw that broke the camel's back was when another classmate of mine, who was a senior, came up missing. His car was parked in the school parking lot, but he was nowhere to be found. At the end of that week, the police decided to search his car for clues, and found his body in the trunk. He had been shot in the head; it was said that it was a drug deal gone bad.

Before my mother transferred me to St. Willibrord, I enrolled in driver's ed, which was a breeze since my brother taught me how to drive when I was ten. There was even a time when my brother had too much to drink and made me drive us home. Of course, he warned me before putting me behind the wheel of his car that if I wrecked it, he was going to wreck my face. I managed to get us home, and my brother gave me a rare compliment. "Good job, I guess you are not such a screw up after all." I flew through driver's ed, and it was so easy for me that they had me helping to train other students. I got my permit and couldn't wait until my 16th birthday. My mother made a deal with me: she would match whatever I saved toward a car. So, I worked any and all jobs I was able to, so that I could save up a nice amount.

By my 16th birthday I had saved up one hundred and eighty dollars. My next-door neighbor Michael was an Illinois state trooper and was really laid back and smooth. He used to smoke weed with my brother, which really blew my mind because he was a state trooper. I always used to admire his 1973 Buick Riviera. It had a dent in the driver's side door, and it needed a muffler, but other than that it was so nice. It was brown with a boat tail and looked like a black man's Batmobile.

My mother one day asked, "Do you like Mike's car?"

I said, "Mike next door?"

"Yes."

I just smiled and nodded yes frantically. I knew how fast the car was and just thought about how awesome it would be to cruise in it. My mother and I went and checked it out. Mike took one look at me and said, "This car is for him?" I looked at him like, *shut up man, don't blow this for me!* He said, "I don't know, do you know how fast this car is?" Mike wasn't so cool to me anymore at that moment, I had to beg my mother to buy the car. My brother was my actual saving grace, when he spoke to my mother. I don't know what he said but after speaking with him, she agreed to buy the car. I had to wait for the registration because the title to the car was messed up and my mother said I couldn't drive it until I saved up enough money to get a muffler put on it. It sat in my backyard, where I admired it, washed it, and dreamed of the day I could drive it. My friends would come over, and we would fix little things wrong with it. I had one friend at St. Willibrord who wanted to become an auto mechanic, and like me, he knew a lot about cars.

I learned a lot about them by working on Terrence's cars with him in Streamwood. He had a knack for working on cars and even took the engine out of an orange 1973 Nova and put a racing motor in it and changed it into a stick shift. This car was fast! It had a 350 engine that my brother put in it, with a Holley four-barrel carburetor. My brother bragged about this car a lot, to the point that he told one guy, "My little brother could beat you in my car."

The guy bet my brother, and my brother pulled me to the side to give me a "pep" talk. Basically, he reminded me of how to drive the car and told me he would kill me if I lost the race or wrecked his car. Because I feared my brother, I took his words to heart. My brother lined the car up for the race then shoved me behind the wheel with a menacing look. I don't think the guy dropped his hat good before I punched it, barely keeping control of the car as it fishtailed and slid from side to side. I was able to keep the car straight enough to win, but I couldn't stop the damn thing and slid into a pole, damaging the front right bumper of the car.

Looking back, I saw my brother running top speed toward me and his car. I wanted to get out and run for my life, but I was a little dizzy and by the time I got out of the car, he was already face-to-face with me. He ducked inside of his car and turned it off before grabbing me and asking me if I was okay. I stuttered yes, and he started yelling, "That's my little brother! I told you!"

I assumed they raced title for title because that guy's car showed up at my house, and my brother sold it. My brother later flipped that Nova in a cornfield somewhere in Streamwood, which I knew was hard for him because he loved that car so much.

The day came when I got the registration for my car, and my mother said she would help get an exhaust for it. I think she offered to help because St. Willibrord was in a bad neighborhood, and we would have to fight kids from the surrounding public schools on the way to school and on the way home. My mother had heard several different stories, like when a classmate of mine was robbed and then picked up and thrown through an open window of a CTA bus while the bus was moving on the way to school. He was wearing his uniform sweater, which made him a target.

The trick was not to wear anything on the street that indicated you went to St. Willibrord. Once you got to school, you could put it on. Not only did he not listen, but he chose to sit in the back of the bus instead of standing where it was safe in the front. I am not saying he deserved what happened to him, but there were ways to avoid confrontation.

I was able to save enough to get a dual exhaust, which was cheaper. The reason this was significant was because dual exhaust made the car sound cooler, and let the engine breathe better, which led to a little more speed. I nervously drove the car to school the first day, not knowing if the kids were going to crack jokes because of the dent in the door or what. Kids are so unpredictable, and I had received so much negativity, that my thoughts shifted to negativity first, versus a positive response. But what happened was not only a surprise but extremely positive. I got so many compliments from freshmen, sophomores, and seniors! I couldn't believe it. I was finally considered one of the cool kids. Gavin had a lot of friends at this school, and I was already part of the "in-crowd" because I was his sidekick. But this was different. I slowly began to get notoriety of my own!

This car was so powerful and fast that one time it got me out of a jam that almost cost me my life! A classmate and I were talking in front of my car on the southside when we heard, "There goes that mother f@#r right there!" At first it sounded like firecrackers down the block, then I heard something that sounded like a HUGE bee whisk past my ear. My classmate screamed, "They're shooting!" and dove headfirst through the window-opening of my car. I jumped through the driver's window-opening and, in what seemed to be one full motion, had the car started and in gear. When I punched the gas, it looked like something out of a *Fast and Furious* movie. There was a wall of smoke behind my car from burning so much rubber. We later found out from the neighborhood that it was a case of mistaken identity. Gavin was a really good guy and people flocked to him. He was very laid back and had this swagger that girls loved and guys gravitated toward.

It was rare for a sophomore to have their own car. The girls flocked, and between Gavin's popularity and my car, I guess I was now one of the cool guys. I began to carry myself differently and had a newfound confidence. I also found out that girls showed a lot of appreciation for rides home, if you know what I mean. With this new swagger, I became someone else that I hid behind. This new person has always caused me issues, but I realize now God was ALWAYS present. This new person I became was still very naïve, and without God I don't know how some situations would have played out. One of many examples of that is when Gavin and I watched the news one night. A story came on about a guy who the streets hailed as a hero, but the law hailed as a gangster and a terrorist.

A search warrant was executed on a local place called "The Fort" where they found multiple military grade weapons, which included hand grenades, were seized. A short while after that I began paying attention to a young lady in school that everyone seemed to respect and like. I could understand why she was liked because she was so full of energy, fun and cool. We joked around whenever we saw each other, and I began to wonder how far things could go. I told Gavin about my interest in her, and Gavin looked at me like I had a third leg growing out of my butt. I was slow to understand who she was because of her physical attributes, and she was friendly, and fun, but Gavin brought me back to that day we watched the news. He made me realize that she was the daughter of the co-founder of one of the major gangs in Chicago. I snapped to my senses pretty quick after that and stayed friendly with her but gave up any further pursuit of her. Later I saw her take down a girl twice her size in the hallway between classes. It was so quick and effortless. As quick as the fight started, it was over.

I began to learn things about myself, like the fact that I didn't really care about fitting in with the "in-crowd," was not true. Once I started fitting in it felt good to fit in. In contrast, I had gotten used to walking to the beat of my own drum and being my own person. I would rebel against the "in-crowd" when it came to them picking on or making fun of those who were not with the "in-crowd." I would stick up for those that couldn't or didn't stick up for themselves and try to comfort them and build their self-esteem. I remembered how it felt, and I could sympathize with them. I wasn't totally in the "in-crowd" because I was still odd even though accepted. Even when I laughed at a joke about someone, that may have been funny, God would deal with my heart, which would cause me to try to make up for it by correcting the person telling the joke or being demeaning. I would also comfort the person being hurt or bullied.

I didn't know it at the time, but this was attractive to the unpopular girls, who, in turn, became very friendly. They were even more interesting than the regular girls. The unpopular girls were more receptive and open-minded. Even some of the popular girls found me attractive when I stood up for others. I wish I had put the energy into school that I put into fitting in, and into girls. I was an average student, but I could have been an above average student. I had this dream of having just one serious girlfriend that I could grow with and build a bond with. I had these ideas that started forming in my head at an early age.

I used my mother's love as a guide to help me form this checklist in my head. I wanted a girl that would be a true partner, and push me, when I wasn't pushing myself, to be the best me. In turn I would push her to be the best she could be, and together we would be the power couple in life, business, and family. I have had this dream since I was ten years old. I guess I began to change when my heart was broken, and my expectations were smashed over and over again like a fragile piece of china in a store with a bull running loose in it. This heartbreak happened time after time in life as heartbreak does, but sometimes you have to go through the good to get to the bad. Regardless, God was there even in the heartbreak.

CHAPTER ELEVEN

HUMBLENESS VERSUS PRIDE

Keep your friends close and your enemies closer

When I broke up with Keshia in 1987, I met a girl that I fell head over heels with named Dawn. It was love at first sight! I was at Gavin's house, when from across the street this gorgeous dark complected girl came out on her front porch. She had long black hair that came down past her shoulders, with these beautiful soft brown eyes and lips that looked like they were made for kissing. She had an athletic body, and she was wearing a blue button-down shirt tied at the bottom, showing off her bellybutton. Her jeans looked painted on, and she had a smile that would make you forget everything around you. Gavin introduced us and I was hooked. We were thick as thieves until she betrayed me in a way I didn't see coming! I formed a grudge against her because I let her into my most inner being, and she did the unthinkable. We broke up but stayed friends. It was hard to remove someone who was so entrenched in my soul.

I eventually forgave Dawn, and Dawn forgave me. I treated Dawn really bad. I loved her but I was hurt. When I met Denisha, I had turned into this so-called player, who still held this secret dream in his heart. Denisha, "Denny" was beautiful inside and out. She was also a virgin when I met her. I thought she had everything on my checklist to be the girl I had been looking for since I was ten years old, but I was damaged. She was light complected, with long beautiful hair and a smile that could slay a dragon. She was 5'6" with the personality of a giant! She had an athletic body, and she was on her high school dance team. It wasn't long before I fell head over heels for her.

We would talk for hours on the phone. And even though we both had to get up early for school, we wouldn't hang up, sometimes sleeping while holding the phone. She gave me ego boosts that, like my mother's, made me believe I could do anything. Denny trusted me with her heart and, eventually, with her body and her virginity. I moved slowly with her, enjoying the days and nights of being in her company. The day I took her virginity I knew I had a huge responsibility in being her first. I loved her wholeheartedly and unconditionally, but even though I tried to hide it behind my macho attitude, I was damaged and flawed.

My senior year, my mother couldn't afford the tuition at St. Willibrord, which had combined with two other schools and became St. Martin de Porres. I wound up at a public school called Bowen on the southeast side of Chicago. This school was also in a poor neighborhood and had a reputation at the time of being a rough school. My first day there, I observed how it was not like the private schools I'd gone to. In the private schools everything was more or less done undercover. I was used to organization and a more disciplined atmosphere. But here the atmosphere was more of a rowdy ruckus.

There was one instance where I put my books that I didn't need in my locker and turned around to go to class. As I tried to cross the hallway, a student was playing around and started chasing another student. I inadvertently stepped in his way and cut him off. When he stopped short, a

38 revolver fell from under his sweatshirt and landed on the floor right between us. We both looked down at the gun—and then at each other. I quickly did my best impression of Ray Charles and walked away as he quickly picked up the gun and went the opposite way. On a separate incident, I found myself surrounded by five kids, because I refused to be a target.

One of the kids found out I'd gone to private school and decided that I was an easy mark. My brother always taught me two things. One, guard my space. You don't let people into your personal space. He taught me to set a boundary and, if they stepped beyond that boundary, take action. Second, in a situation like this, take out the mouth. Usually, the main one speaking is pumped up because he has followers that are ready to back him up.

The kid was loud and animated. He kept walking toward me, and as he did, I warned him not to walk up to me. I don't know if that was a mistake or not, but it seemed to spark this kid and he stepped beyond my personal boundary screaming, "What you going to do!" I looked around and knew I was outnumbered and outmatched. I don't even think he fully finished his sentence before I grabbed him and spun him around in a choke hold. I went down to the ground choking him, knowing that his entourage was going to attack me. They began punching, stomping, and kicking me. I tucked my head in close to his to protect my face as best as I could. I tightened my grip around his neck. He began gasping for air because the more they kicked, punched, and stomped me, the tighter I clenched around his neck. I started yelling, "He is going to die!" One of them heard him gasping and making these choking noises and told everyone to stop. I yelled, "Back up, back up!"

They backed up, but I knew the attack would begin again as soon as I let him go. I yelled, "Make a hole!" The guy I was choking went limp in my grip. They made a hole, and when I saw the opening, I dropped him and made a run for it. While I was running, I began praying. "Jesus, please help me; I think he is dead! I am going to jail!" As I came to the corner, I looked back. The guy I had been choking had slightly rolled to one side and looked like he was trying to get up as his entourage tried helping him. I was so relieved. Once again, I had to adapt and try to be in the background and not draw attention to myself. I just wanted to make it to graduation and move on. Five months before graduation, there was something that changed all of that.

For Christmas, Denny bought me this Eddie Bauer bookbag that was very popular. It was a huge fashion statement, I guess, and everybody wanted one. I didn't want to even take it to school and use it as my school book bag, I was only going to use it on special occasions because it was so nice! Denny said she had bought it to be used and she would be hurt if I didn't use it every day. Against my better judgment, I put my books in it and took it to school. Toward the end of the first day that I took the book bag to school, this kid who was in my class started making conversation with me. I turned to answer his question; I took my eye off my book bag that was sitting on my desk for one second. Within that second, I turned back around, and my book bag was gone, along with my books that were in it. I was not only beyond angry but totally confused. It happened so quickly! Was this a joke someone was playing on me? When I told Denny about it, she could not believe it either. She was very calm about it but hurt.

The next day, we were lined up outside of the school doors, waiting for them to let us in and begin the school day. The kid who asked me a question at the end of class the day before, was standing across from me laughing and joking with some of his friends in our class. He and his friends made me feel like I was the butt of whatever jokes were being told. As I stared over at him, I noticed that he had a brand-new Eddie Bauer bookbag that he did not have before.

I approached him and said, "Man, that is a nice book bag!"

He replied, "Yeah, I just picked it up!"

As he laughed and looked back at his friends, I asked if I could check it out, and he agreed. While he tightly held the handles of the book bag, I looked behind the Eddie Bauer tag. I looked back at the kid and said, "Man, this is my book bag, and we can do this one of two ways: I can kick your butt and take my bag back, or we can go to the principal's office!"

To my shock, he wanted to go to the principal's office and repeated, "This is my bag!"

We went straight to the office. The principal, who looked exhausted and like he really didn't want to be bothered, said, "So what's going on here?"

I calmly stated that just the day prior someone had stolen my book bag, and that this kid had it. I went on to say that he had diverted my attention by asking me a question, and one of his friends must have swiped it then. The kid became animated and raised his voice, stating that he did not steal anything and it was his book bag. The principal, who had the bag on his desk, asked me in an annoyed voice, "How do you know that this is your book bag?"

I asked to see the bag and, when he handed it to me, flipped the Eddie Bauer tag over and showed it to him. As I did, I said, "Do you see the initials there? Unless his initials are POH this is MY book bag!"

The principal seemed to be shocked and impressed at the same time. He looked at the kid and said, "You know what this means for you, right?"

The kid dropped his head as he said, "Yeah." The principal asked what he did with my books, and the kid said he threw them in the garbage. The principal handed me my book bag and told me to go to class.

I felt vindicated and accomplished, but that quickly turned to concern. This kid was a serious problem child and, because of this incident, was expelled from school. His parents were held liable for my school books. Part of me didn't care, but the other part was asking, *What did I just do?* This kid ranked high in the Latin Kings, the third major gang on Chicago's east side, and I had confronted and embarrassed him in front of his crew. According to the rumors around school, he was now gunning for me.

My mother began dropping me off at school because she didn't want me catching the bus with this threat over my head. We were sitting in front of the school one morning, and she asked me if I had lunch money. I said no, and she began digging in her purse. While she was doing that, I noticed that kids were running towards us. They scattered, and behind them was the kid that had it in for me. He ran up and noticed me sitting in the car. As we made direct eye contact, I noticed something that made me tell my mother to back the car up. I began repeating, "Mom, back the car up! Mom, back the car up," to the point I was yelling. She looked to see what was going on, saw what I saw, and quickly began backing up. The kid was standing there, staring, a menacing look on his face, and a gun in his hand.

I believe that God had my mother and I covered because he ran off without shooting at my mother's car. My mother asked if that was the boy that got expelled and had the grudge, and I told her yeah, that was him. My mother pulled off and said, "You won't be going to school today." About an hour after we got back home, she told me she wanted to talk to me. She began trying to convince me to drop out and get my GED. I argued, saying I wanted to graduate, and I didn't want a GED because it was looked down upon. I tried going back to school, but every day, I was threatened and told by his friends that he was coming. Rumors began spreading around school, and I became known as "the dead man walking." My mother stressed the point that she didn't want anything to happen to me.

I eventually agreed to taking my GED and went on to take the test, passing it on the first try, without even studying for it. I kept it secret from everyone including Denny. I was amazed that Denny was able to see through my bravado and love me in spite of those flaws and push me past the low expectations I had for myself. But even with that, I was still too embarrassed to tell her.

My life took another turn when I learned that my "friends" were not true "friends." I had fallen into hanging with the wrong crowds. This crowd was completely different from the friend I had in Gavin. Where Gavin was laid-back and reluctant to get in trouble, this crowd was a group of troublemakers that didn't have any fear about crossing the line. The so-called friend that I met Denny through went to school with me. He was an outcast. Like I said earlier, I stood up for and hung around those that didn't "fit in" to the norm. But this particular person had ties that, at the time, I was too naïve to understand. His friends were well-connected gang members. Those friends quickly became my friends; one of them had a father who was serving a six-life-sentence term! Another one of the crew was someone who kept me out of the street gang when I wanted to join this "family." He invited me to an initiation, and what I saw instantly changed my mind.

He told me to meet him at an open baseball field at 7am that Saturday morning. I remember thinking "damn that's early!" He said to meet him there and we would talk about how to get into the "family." That summer Saturday morning, I struggled to get up. As I was on my way to the baseball field, I began to take in the day. The sun was shining, the birds were chirping, and the temperature was just right. I got to the open empty field thinking; he is trying to make a fool out of me. There is no one here. As I got closer there was a set of bleachers, and there at the top of the bleachers was my "friend." I went to go to the top of the bleachers to meet him and to start asking him a load of questions that raced through my mind. Before I could, he told me to sit on the bottom bleacher. Shortly after I sat down, this guy walked up and sat down next to me. I asked him if he knew what was going on. He nervously looked at me and said, "you will see."

The next thing I know, all of these hard looking dudes started walking up as others were getting out of their cars. They started throwing gang signs as they greeted each other and showing each other love. I sat in nervous amazement as they filled the open field, and the guy next to me stood up. I looked back to the top of the bleacher at my friend, he glanced down at the guy standing next to me. He gives him a head nod and with that the guy standing next to me tells me to wish him luck. I didn't say a word as I sat wondering what the hell was going on!

He walked out to the middle of the field and with one whistle from my friend, the guy that was just standing next to me asking me to wish him luck, disappeared into a barrage of fists from everywhere. They punched and kicked this guy to the point it looked like they were trying to hammer him into the dirt. My friend stood up and whistled again, and yelled "alright, that's enough! Now show him some love!" They picked this guy up off the ground and he looked like a wet shirt ready to be hung to dry.

They hugged him, and told him welcome into the family, you are one of us now. As they helped him back over to the bleacher where I was still sitting with my mouth hanging open, I looked back at my friend. My friend came down from the top of the bleachers and through his arm around my shoulder. He said, "So this is how you get in, do you want to go next?" I said, "HELL NO!!!" I could fight even though I didn't like to, but to be swarmed, stomped, kicked and punched until someone else says stop?! It literally not only sobered me up to the reality of the fact that I was not as hard as I thought, but that this may not actually be a life that I wanted. With a loud chuckle, he told me something I didn't understand at the time. He told me that there was more out there for me, and to pursue it.

About a month later he was shot and killed. He was standing out in front of this fast-food restaurant that was on a busy street known for violence on the southside of Chicago waiting on a food order to get done. A car with someone he knew from the neighborhood pulled up on the busy street in front of the restaurant. He was from a rival gang and threw up his sign at my friend. My friend threw his sign back up. The dude put his car in park and told my friend to do it again. It is said he had a girl in the car with him that he was trying to impress. My friend threw his gang sign again and the dude that was driving the car pulled a 22 pistol out from the trunk of his car and shot my friend once in the chest. He was trying to get help and collapsed 3 blocks away, where they found his body. I went to his funeral and as I stood over his coffin, I replayed the conversation in my head about how there was a better future for me. As I shed tears of sadness, I whispered to him that I would do better.

My friend who was killed, although involved in gang activity, still had my back and tried to watch out for me. However, a former classmate or "so-called friend" who introduced me to the new crowd did not have my best interest at heart. This so-called friend introduced me to Denny. Little did I know, he was jealous of the relationship that Denny and I had and interfered in it. Denisha was a *definite* weak spot. We spent so much time together that it was not even funny. I *thought* I had so much to teach her, but instead, I had *so* much to learn. She was only 16 years old, and I was going on 18.

One of the things that I learned about myself is that I am a hopeless romantic. I scraped money together and bought Denisha an engagement/promise ring. My former classmate told me I was stupid and tried talking me out of giving it to her, but I wasn't listening to anything that he had to say. I presented Denny with the ring and asked her to be my future wife. I was met with nervous laughter and an immediate no, not right now. I didn't mean right there and then; I meant in the future. I guess in my naiveness, I thought with this ring that I could get some type of committed guarantee. I didn't realize I was being selfish. Denisha was too young and hadn't even experienced life yet. Her reply was logical, but it was not the reply that I anticipated or wanted.

Because I was young, immature, and damaged, I didn't think about that and felt rejected. I have always been a loner and I felt I needed to guard my feelings. I did the unthinkable and started cheating on her. I did to Denny exactly what was done to me. Denny caught me red handed. You see, by the time that our relationship came to an end I was living up north with a roommate in my own apartment. I was about 22 and she was about 20. She was spending more and more time with her friends hanging out and living life. I felt like we were not as close as we used to be and that she did not want to spend as much time together. She still lived on the southside while I now lived on the far northside. She unexpectedly dropped by my apartment one day while Dawn was there. Dawn was still in love with me and didn't care that I was in a relationship with Denny because her goal was to win me back.

I could see the front gate from my apartment window, and when the bell rang, I froze! It was Denny with one of her friends. Instead of buzzing the gate to let her into the courtyard I began to panic. I began thinking, ok I will wait for her to leave and then race her from my apartment back to her grandmothers and pretend I wasn't home and that I was at her grandmothers looking for her. Denny never bought that story even though I did in fact beat her to her grandmother's house. Her suspicions were confirmed when the so-called friend/classmate went to her and her family behind my back and told them everything. He even made some stuff up to be sure that there was no way that Denny would ever forgive me.

To this day I regret that choice, and it took me a long time to take accountability for my actions. I broke her heart. I also learned that you have to be careful, because not *everyone* who calls themselves your friend is your friend. The so-called friend / classmate that embedded himself in the middle of our relationship wanted Denisha for himself, even though he was the one that introduced us. I took ownership of my actions and gave the classmate/friend the fuel that he needed to blow the relationship up. But the lies he told on top of the truth is what gets me the most.

By breaking Denisha's heart, I broke mine. It changed me, unfortunately too late. Denisha, her family, and my family were so disappointed in me, and I was honestly disappointed in myself. My roommate and friend was Dawn's brother. He moved her into our apartment and then just told me, "she will be staying here for awhile." I wound up eventually getting back together with Dawn. I tried putting my best foot forward in being a good man, however I still did not know what that was. I eloped with Dawn. I went to visit my family who had all gathered at my mother's condo. This was a normal thing that usually happened after church on Sundays. I was sitting at my mother's dining room table when I broke the news that Dawn, and I eloped and that she now had a new daughter-in-law. My mother laughed at first and said, "I know you are kidding right?" When I said "no, I am serious," my mother tried to jump across the table to grab me. My mother, my sister, and both of my brothers were beyond upset. They all felt I was not ready to be married.

I worked while Dawn went to school. She originally went to school to become a nurse, but lost interest in it. I wanted to continue to support her until she figured out what exactly she wanted to do but at the time she didn't know what that was. Dawn began to change drastically, to the point that one day I came home from playing basketball on my off day and while she was finishing dinner said, "I don't want to do this anymore, this cooking, cleaning thing is not me." Eventually, I helped her get a receptionist position with a major company on the Northside of Chicago. We began to have issues just like Denny and I did, with everyone having a say so in our marriage and relationship. I remember going to church one Sunday and after church trying to talk to my mother about what was going on. My mother cut me off and said, "you made your bed now lay in it!" I was immature at the time and didn't know how to navigate my decisions properly. Everything that had gone on with Dawn was not handled well at all. It was at that moment my life took a turn down a dark valley. Even in the valley of death, God was with me.

CHAPTER TWELVE

LOST IN PAIN, SORROW, AND GRIEF.

One day you feel like you've lost something but have no clue what you lost.

Then one day you realize what you lost is yourself"

My heart shattered. My heart ached, and I felt pain like never before. In early 1995, my oldest brother, Gerald, had just gotten married. Everyone from my immediate family was gathered at his house for a BBQ. I have loved family gatherings since I was a kid. They were always filled with so much love. But this family gathering had an ending that would leave my siblings and I stressed. My mother made an announcement that she tried to keep casual, but everyone quickly figured out that it was not a casual announcement. My mother, who was the rock of the family, said that she was going in for tests regarding ulcers that she had developed in the mid '80s. She said they were back and causing pain when she ate, but that this was an exploratory procedure that was just routine and nothing to worry about. We all asked a lot of questions that were met with: "It's nothing to worry about" and "It will be okay."

My mother went in for those tests that Tuesday, with the family in attendance in the waiting room. I paced back and forth, wearing out the rug underneath my feet. The doctor came out and called the family into a consultation room. He sighed and cleared his throat. "Your mother has colon cancer," he said in a voice that was low and somber but echoed through my brain. He went on to say that when they did the exploratory procedure, they found that the cancer had spread rapidly.

A few months prior to this, I had renewed my relationship with God, and my mother was so happy about it. It was one of the outcomes that came from my broken ego and heart. I realized and remembered who was actually *always* there for me, guiding me and protecting me. I had spoken to him daily when I was a kid, and I realized that he was still there.

I began praying for my mother day and night. It seemed the more I prayed the better she got. In less than a week she was home from the hospital and getting stronger.

We brought her home and got her comfortable. I stayed by her side the entire time. We reminisced about my childhood and the good times. I also apologized for the problems that I gave her

Listed from left; my brother Terrence, my Mom, and Me.

growing up, like the time when I was 14 and I stepped out of line, and my mother bit me. We laughed about that, and I told her that I thought she was crazy. With this sly grin on her face, she asked, "How else do you think I kept you boys in line?"

The doctors wanted to start chemo on her within the next week, and it was starting to get late. At about midnight, I reluctantly got up off the floor next to her bed. I had been there because I wanted to be as close to her as possible without lying in bed with her. She tried to start a conversation with me about how proud she was of me. I was 23, I had my own apartment. I had never been to jail and was holding down a job and taking care of myself. I remember getting upset when she made a statement about not being around in the near future. I said to her, "why are we even having this discussion?! You are not going anywhere so I don't want to talk about that!"

I had this ritual with her whenever I greeted her or left her. I would kiss her on the forehead. The joke between us was that she was 5'3" and I was 6'3", and she would always say, "I need to climb up there to knock you in your head now. But you are never too tall to get knocked down!" So, my kiss to her forehead was an affectionate bow and joke all in one.

On July 5, I spoke to my mother on the phone. She asked, "When are you coming back to see me?" I lived on the far north side of Chicago, and she lived in the far south suburbs of Chicago. By this time, I worked for a greeting card company doing commercial collections. It was an easy job that involved reconciling invoices and payments to clear account discrepancies. I made a modest salary, and I was on a tight budget. I told her I had just enough gas to make it back and forth to work until payday.

She said that if I could make it to her house, she would fill my gas tank and give me a little money. She also said that my brother Terrence had just been there to get some money. I became infuriated and growled at my mother saying, "I am not Terrence!" I was angry at the fact that my mother was now on a fixed income, but my brother was there getting money from her. My mother laughed and said, "No you are not Terrence, you are going to be ok, you are going to be ok." She said, "Okay, baby, don't wait too long!"

On July 6, I got up with a horrible feeling that something was wrong somewhere, but I had just spoke to my mother the night before, and she was okay. I generally spoke to my mother on a regular basis and several times throughout each day. I called my mother to talk to her about the bad feeling that I was having, but her phone line was busy. That was really odd because she had call-waiting, but I figured maybe everyone was calling her to encourage her and see how she was doing. I got to work and settled in behind my desk. As I began my day at work, I continued trying to call my mother. In between trying to get some work done, I continued to call and get a busy signal. I decided to call my brother, Terrence's job. When I called his job, they said that he had left early.

I then decided to call my sister-in-law's job because I was wondering where Terrence was. When I called her job, they said that she left early due to a family emergency; the person I was speaking to put me on hold. My sister-in-law's boss got on the phone and asked, "Who am I speaking with?"

I said, "My name is Phillip. I am her brother-in-law."

With a pause and hesitation that felt like an eternity, she said somberly, "I am so sorry Phillip, but the family emergency is … that your mother … She passed."

I hung up on her and immediately called my mother's number again, because she had it wrong. The phone finally rang instead of giving me a busy signal. I expected my mother to answer, but instead it was my sister. She said, "You need to get here as soon as possible."

I said, "Why?" She got quiet, and I said, "I think I know."

Fighting back tears, she said, "Yeah, you know."

I shared a large and heavy maple wood executive-style desk with a person sitting to my left. I still remember the shock on not only his face but everyone's in the room when I reacted. It was a look of sheer terror from him and pure shock from everyone else. I stood up from the desk, grabbed the edge of it where I was sitting, and flipped it completely over as I screamed, "NNNNOOOOO!!!!"

As I stormed toward the door, I looked my manager in the face with a stare that horrified her. The rage and pain I felt were unbearable. I felt like the Incredible Hulk because even though it wouldn't change the news I just got, all I wanted to do was break and smash. At this time, I drove a 1991 Chevy Cavalier Z24. I jumped into my car, and because it was a front-wheel-drive, the smoke that came from those tires made it hard to see where I was going. As I barreled down the street, a couple of guys were crossing in front of me against the light. I had to make the green because I *had* to get to my mother. They saw me coming and one ran, while the other kind of slowed his pace like he was going to take his time.

I smashed the gas even harder as he jumped out of the way, cursing at me. I slammed on the breaks, sliding to a screeching stop. I went to the trunk of my car and pulled out a baseball bat. He was walking toward me, as I was walking toward him, when his friend grabbed him and said, "Come on, let's go, he doesn't seem right."

His friend took a second look at me and stopped. He went from an angry look to a puzzled and concerned look. His friend screamed at him, "LETS GO!"

I raised the bat, pointing it at him as I loudly growled, "You better listen to your friend because if you don't, I am going to hit a home run WITH YOUR HEAD!" He turned toward his friend and began to quickly walk away as I threw the bat back into the trunk of my car. I turned my attention back to trying to turn my car into a rocket ship. I didn't and couldn't believe that she was gone. I had to prove that everyone was lying. *When I get to her, she is going to still be there!* I kept thinking, *no, this cannot be true! I just spoke to her, she was FINE!*

I turned an hour drive from the North Side of Chicago to the South suburbs of Chicago into a 28-minute time warp. When I arrived, I barely parked. I ran as fast as I could to the second-floor condo my mother lived in. I got to the door and almost broke my key in the lock trying to get in. I got in and immediately looked around for any sign that she was still there alive. All I found were my brothers and my sister answering phone calls and consoling each other. I went into my mother's bedroom, and on the floor was just garbage from the paramedics, and the covers from my mother's bed. My mother was not there, she was … Gone!

The doctors suspected that my mother had had a blood clot in her leg, and that when she stood up early on July 6, the clot shot to her heart and killed her instantly. They said that she died before she hit the floor. My niece, who was staying with her to help her with her recovery, heard something at about 3 a.m. but didn't know what it was. She thought it may have been one of the neighbors and went back to sleep. It was at this point that I began to spiral. We had planned a surprise birthday for our mother because her birthday was July 8. She would have been 61 years old. I demanded an answer from God! WHY? My brothers, my sister, and I went to make arrangements. The first time I saw my mother again was when we had to approve her body for the funeral. Terrence tried his best to prepare me and support me, but when I saw her something inside literally just … shattered. I felt like I wasn't getting an answer from God, and I felt alone.

After the funeral I fell into a very deep depression. My mother had been my mother, my father, and my best friend.

I told God that I wasn't speaking to him anymore, and with that I stopped. As I found myself spinning and spiraling, I didn't care! Dawn tried to do everything in her power to be there for me and console me, but nothing worked. Dawn got pregnant which was a highpoint, but my mother wouldn't be there to see her born. I fell back into my old immature ways, and well like they say hurt people, hurt people. I did not treat Dawn very well at all. Even during the pregnancy all the way up and till she gave birth. When I held that little girl, it touched me in a way that scared the hell out of me. I never had a father and didn't know anything about being one. I tried to make it work between me and Dawn but, with all of the negative opinions being hurled at me from every direction about me, it came to a boiling point for me. I eventually left.

CHAPTER THIRTEEN

NAVIGATION WITHOUT A COMPASS

Without God, getting lost is easy.

In 1996 I tried to drown my pain with any and everything I could, with the exception of drugs. I made things worse by trying to fill the void with a relationship and wound up in a marriage that I had NO business being in. This woman, who we'll call Carmen, joked about being the devil's daughter, and it got to the point that I believed it wasn't a joke. We started off as a "friends with benefits," relationship. A relationship that was supposed to be all fun, sex, and games with no serious commitment. I hated to be doubted! I had become this man that took it to heart that actions speak louder than words, because you can make your mouth say anything. I showed her that I loved her and I said it as well. She picked up on the fact that I hate to be doubted and manipulated it to her advantage. If she wanted me to do something she would always lead with, *"If you loved me you'd do this or that."*

I dated her for a year before leaving her. I think the excitement from the out of the norm style of the relationship I was used to began to wear off. Not to mention the fact of how she treated me like dirt. We stayed in an apartment that was just outside downtown Chicago. I was lost and still dealing with the loss of my mother. I was still trying to pull myself together. I was in-between jobs and didn't have bus fare to get a job interview located in downtown Chicago and back. I asked her for bus fare to get to the job interview and she told me to get on my knees and beg her for it.

I was in total disbelief and refused. I wound up walking over an hour and a half back from the job interview plotting how after getting my first paycheck I would leave. I took that first check and left her. After a year we wound up getting back together. I can't really tell you how it happened. I know I was still lost but doing better than I was. I was still in finance/collections at the time when one day I was sitting at my desk thinking about my mother. I remember my mother telling me that I needed to get into computers. She insisted that computers were the future, and I would be good at computers. I completed my assigned work and was bored. My mother's words echoed in my head, so I began looking at different things on the computer at my desk.

The IT department supposedly removed the internet from everyone's computer at work. I saw the internet explorer icon on the desktop and began thinking, I thought they removed this. I began troubleshooting and digging into it. I was able to re-engineer what they did and get on the internet. I kept it a secret until one day I was caught by a nosey coworker. I kept to myself a lot and was surrounded by an all-female department including my boss. My co-worker told me that she wouldn't say anything if I fixed her computer too. I was able to transfer the files needed to make it work from my desktop to hers and get hers to work as well.

Of course, it did not stay secret and one day I was called to my manager's office. My manager was a strong black woman who somewhat reminded me of my sister. My manager confronts me by telling me how good I was with my accounting and collection skills, but that we had a problem. As I swallowed hard, she started asking about what she heard around the office. She said she heard that I was putting the internet on people's machines. I sat there silently waiting to hear "you're fired!" I thought about the fact that I had my own apartment, a car note and lived paycheck to paycheck! What she said next shocked me, she said "you are in a lot of trouble unless you can fix my machine too!" I jumped behind her desk and sat there nervously trying to figure out why what I had done on the other machines had not worked on her machine.

I calmed down and began thinking through what I was doing and was able to figure out why her machine was different from the others. The IT department had been lazy with the other machines and partially uninstalled internet explorer and blocked permissions to reinstall it. With her machine I had to put the files I downloaded on a network shared drive and login as administrator to do a complete install. I overheard two IT employees talking and quickly wrote down the password that one IT employee gave to the other. It took me longer than the other machines, but I was able to get it working. She looks at me and says "wow!" She then proceeds to pick up the phone and call the IT Manager into her office. I said to her "I thought you said if I fixed it, I wouldn't be in trouble, I need this job!" The IT manager comes in and my manager asks, "I thought you removed the internet from all of the machines?" The IT manager exclaims, "I did!" My manager smirks at me as she turns her screen around and says, "so how was my employee able to get on the internet?"

At this point I began wondering how I was going to pay my rent, and the fact that I just paid all of my bills, which meant I had about a month to find another job before I was out on the street. The IT manager looked completely confused as he sat behind the keyboard and figured out what I did. He gets frustrated and begins asking me questions as to what I did which I gave half answers to. The IT manager called one of his employees into my manager's office and together we began speaking a lot of computer jargon. The employee tells the IT manager, "I don't know how he figured this out, but he is good." The IT manager agreed as he laughed with amazement. As the IT manager and his employee were about to leave, the IT manager said jokingly, "maybe he should come and work for me."

My manager just smiles and says, "you need to remove the internet from everyone's computer except mine." After they left her office, feeling angry, but nervous I stood up and said, "I will go clean out my desk!" I felt like she lied to me and now she was going to fire me.

What she said next blew my mind, she said" sit down, you're not fired, yet!" Confused, I sat back down. She goes on to ask, "are you happy doing this job?"

Before I could answer she said, "I don't think so, I think you are comfortable, but this is not what you should be doing. You are not fired, however you need to go and find a job in IT." She said that she was only going to let me stay for a little longer before she would fire me because I should be doing more with my skills, and she wasn't going to allow me to waste them. I went out and bought some training books, namely the MCSE training books. I went through them and learned the computer lingo and taught myself by repeating hands on what the books said. It had been about a month since my boss told me that she was going to follow through with her threat to fire me. I cut myself off from the world which included friends, and family. I immersed myself into these books, I found the books interesting, and I was hungry and eager to learn more each day. One day at work I get a frantic phone call from Gavin.

"Man, you are not going to believe this!" he said. "Your ex-girlfriend Carmen, got all of my credit information, including my mother and my sisters. She said that if I contacted you and got you to call her so you all could talk, she would give me all of the information that she got!" I could hear the concern in Gavin's voice. I remember telling Gavin when I left my ex Carmen, that "There's going to be one day that she is going to come looking for me, if she contacts you, I don't exist!"

It had been a whole year later, so I was caught off guard and I know Gavin was too, especially with the fact that she pulled the credit files for him and his family. Carmen worked her way back into my life and convinced me she changed. She proposed and like I said earlier, I don't know if it was a void or whole, I was trying to fill or what, but I accepted. Just before she proposed, I landed the very first IT position that I applied for. I did so well in the interview that when I hesitated in taking the position, they offered me a sign on bonus. I hesitated because I was nervous about taking the position and doing well in it.

As the marriage to Carmen progressed, I began weightlifting again to deal with all of the stress from the job and the unhappiness in the marriage to her. My ex did everything she could to extinguish that fire that burnt in everyone filled with hope. She was extremely jealous; she didn't want me talking to *anyone*. Carmen did not have to work because I did so well in my new career. She stayed at home while I worked and took care of her. Eventually, we had two boys born a little less than a year apart. Carmen was a truly hurt, and emotional wreck of a woman, that had a lot of horrible things happen to her throughout her childhood. I used to ask her, "What did I ever do to you?"

She would quickly yell, "It's your fault! You were not supposed to be here, you MADE me fall in love with you!"

Lifting weights was something I started doing when I was 14 years old. I stopped for a while, but then after meeting Carmen, I started again to de-stress. I got up to 315 lbs, but my goal was 325 lbs. I increased my protein intake to increase my mass and size. I got somewhat addicted to the way I felt and looked. My regimen got kind of crazy. I would do a 60-gram protein shake in the morning before I worked out. Then after my workout I would do another 60-gram protein shake. I would get to work, and for lunch I would do another 60-gram protein shake before hitting the gym at work. After my lunchtime workout, I took another 60-gram protein shake.

When I got home from work, I took another 60-gram protein shake and worked out again, ending my night with another 60-gram protein shake. That was 360 grams of protein 5 days a week, and that didn't include the creatine and other supplements.

I got to my goal, but something started happening to me. You see, a few months prior, Carmen and I were in one of those late-night tattoo parlors. We had been drinking and decided to get matching tattoos to proclaim our "love." Something kept telling me NOT to get this tattoo, which would be my second. My first tattoo was a memorial to my mother. It's a Taurus bull standing at the edge of a mountain cliff, looking at the sun setting into the clouds, with a teardrop coming out of its eye.

My zodiac sign is Taurus, so the bull represents me. The sun setting into the clouds represents the passing of my mother, and the teardrop represents my sadness. The bull is standing on the edge of a mountain cliff because I was ready to go over the edge. Carmen kept stressing the point of, "If you love me, prove it, put my name on your chest." I wanted this second tattoo, but I was not getting her name on it. I should have listened to that quiet voice telling me not to get the tattoo, but I didn't. We began arguing as I sat in the chair; the discussion was pretty heated, and I was very aggravated. With all of the commotion I didn't really give thought to the question that I was asked. They said they would give me a discount if they could use a re-sterilized needle.

I answered with a dismissive, "Yeah."

Well, fast forward a few months, and I hit my goal of 325 lbs, but like I said earlier, something was happening to me. I was tired all of the time, and I didn't have the energy I usually had. I also began to have big drops in weight from 325 lbs to 315lbs, from 315lbs to 300lbs. I got all the way back down to 285 lbs before I started really getting concerned. I hadn't changed my protein intake or my workout routine, yet I was still shrinking, and I was lethargic.

Carmen wanted to take out a life insurance policy on me because she didn't work. I took care of her and the kids, and I was the sole source of income. Her logic was that if anything were to happen to me, she wanted to be sure that she and the kids would be taken care of. It made sense to me, so I agreed to it. The life insurance agency came out to the house to do an assessment of my health for the life insurance policy. During the assessment, my energy was at an all-time low. All I wanted to do was sleep. I got up that morning wanting to work out, but I was just too tired. My energy level was so low that I could barely sit up straight and answer the insurance agent's questions. As he went over the policy that

Carmen wanted, I found out that she wanted a $500,000 policy on me. Are you still wondering why she is an ex-wife?

A few days later I received a phone call from the insurance agency informing me that they were not going to approve the half-million-dollar policy, and that I needed to go see a doctor as soon as possible. I went to the doctor, and he informed me that I had hepatitis C. Do you remember that tattoo earlier? Well, the doctors confirmed the re-sterilized needle from that tattoo had hep C contaminated blood in it. Also, the amount of protein that I was doing, along with the creatine, seriously harmed my liver and kidneys. Hep C is what they call a silent killer because it can take years to show any symptoms. Usually, by the time you find out you have the disease, it's already done serious damage that could lead to death.

Because of the stress and damage I was already causing to my liver and kidneys, the symptoms began showing up around a month after getting the tattoo with the re-sterilized needle. Not only did I have hepatitis C, but I had also developed liver cancer from it. The doctors said it was stage 2, and it was possible that I would need a new liver. I suffered several medical issues, including pancreatitis. I went in for a low-risk procedure called an endoscopic retrograde cholangiopancreatography (ERCP), which is a procedure to diagnose and treat problems in the liver, gallbladder, bile ducts, and pancreas. They feed a scope down your throat, through your stomach, and into your small intestine. A small camera mounted on the scope sends a video image to a monitor.

While they were performing the procedure, I woke up from the sedation they had me under. I began fighting with the doctors as they were in my pancreas because I was in so much pain. They eventually got me back under anesthesia, but not before damage was caused to my pancreas. They put me in a medically induced coma while the swelling in my pancreas went down. While I was in the coma, I could hear Carmen on the phone at my bedside with the insurance company, still trying to increase my life insurance policy. My only sister Idelle, who is the oldest, stepped in and took over my care. In 2004 I left Carmen and became a single father. The things that I learned about Carmen during the divorce were outrageous. But I blame myself because I turned my back on God when my mother passed. I had so much pain from the loss of my mother that I would make these off-the-cuff comments about how I wasn't talking to him, and I was mad at him for taking my mother.

My life was chaotic and out of control until, one night, I begged God for mercy and turned back to him. God led me out of that marriage and gave me my peace back! I still had a trail of wreckage around me that I needed to go back and try to repair. One of them being the relationship with my daughter. I felt like I was a tornado and I left an aftermath of hurt, destruction and pain.

PART 3 - MY JOURNEY CONTINUES

CHAPTER FOURTEEN

HE THAT FINDS ...

The annual parade of lights.

I moved forward with my life. The doctors asked that I follow up with them because they wanted to keep an eye on the cancerous tumors that had developed in my liver. In 2006, I had been single for two years after receiving that news, and I was doing great as a bachelor. God blessed me with a new house, I advanced in my career, and I was even back in the gym once again. I got back in the gym after being diagnosed with diabetes in 2005 on top of everything else, but life was good, and God was good to me. Dating hadn't been going so well for me though. I put together a list of what I wanted in a relationship and a partner, and what I did not want. I couldn't understand it. I heard everything from "You are too nice," or "You are too good to be true." A lot of women that weren't interested in anything serious and faulted me because I was. I even had one experience that seriously messed my head up.

For a little while, I had been dating a young lady, who met a lot of things on my list. She was very pretty, we were great friends, and we had a lot of things in common, like shared interests. If I wanted to try something or do something, she was very open-minded and game to try with me. I also tried things that she wanted to try, and I remained open-minded with her. We even made plans to go on vacation together. We were going to go camping, fishing, and to a vintage car show. I was doing some remodeling on my new house, and she came over to help. I needed some things from the hardware store, and she offered to drive. While she was driving, we were laughing and joking around when my cell phone rang. I looked at my phone and saw a number I didn't recognize. I answered it with caution, thinking it was a telemarketer or something. "Hello?"

"Who is this?" The man barked on the other end.

"Who is this?" I barked right back.

He asked me if I knew this woman and began to describe her. The woman he was describing was driving the very car I was riding in. He went on to tell me her name and tell me he was her husband. I made a split-second decision, and thinking quickly, I told him, "Yes, I did a computer repair for her." I had my own computer repair company on the side, and I actually did do an overhaul of her laptop. I didn't want to be in the middle of whatever was going on, but I was beyond pissed. Once her husband and I hung up, I immediately asked her to pull over. We were nowhere near my house, but I was willing to catch the bus or walk home. She insisted that she take me home, and I relented and let her. That was the quietest, and most awkward drive back to my house.

I had a few more dates after that that didn't go well, and I got frustrated. I wasn't the best man out there, but I wasn't the worst. I remember one evening being upset with God and telling him, "Okay, God, I am done! I will just concentrate on my boys and my career." That same

evening on my way to church, I stopped at a Jewel grocery store, because they had a florist, to get some flowers. I wanted to thank the first lady of the church for something nice that she had done for me. On the way, I drove through a parade of fire engines and police cars, all driving with their flashers, sirens, and lights on. I asked the florist what that was all about. Before he could answer I heard a delicate voice from behind me say, "That is the parade of lights." I turned around to see this beautiful young woman. Her smile made my spine tingle, but I was standing firm in what I had just said to God.

I said thank you, and before I could turn back to the florist, she went on to say, "They do it every year. You are not from this area?" I said no, and that I lived in the next suburb over.

She said, "Oh, okay, we'll have a good evening," as she walked away to continue shopping.

The florist, who didn't even know me, said, "Wow, man she was seriously flirting with you."

I looked at him and said, "No, I don't think so."

He said, "Look man, she has been walking back and forth staring and smiling."

I said, "Okay, she is shopping."

He said, "If you don't say something to her, I am going to say something to her for you."

I looked at him and said reluctantly, "If she walks past here again, I will say something."

No sooner had I said that than she walked back by us. The florist looked at me and said, "Well?"

I walked over to this lady who stood 5'3". She was light complected with long hair and these eyes that made my heart melt. "Hi, my name is Phil, what's yours?"

"Tiva," she said with this smile that totally made me forget where I was or what I was doing for a minute. I looked in her basket and asked, "So what's for dinner?"

She responded, "Salad."

With that, I said, "Why don't you let me make you a real dinner?"

She giggled and said, "Okay."

We exchanged numbers and spoke all hours and every chance we got. It was like a whirlwind. Eventually I introduced Tiva to my sons. Collier who was 5 at the time, and Cammeren who was 6. Introducing her to them was a huge deal. Everyone I tried to date before Tiva was always kept away from my boys. My frame of mind was that I didn't want to parade a whole bunch of women in front of them. I wanted to do the best I could do, to present them with stability. Tiva met my boys, and it went off without a hitch. Tiva

introduced me to her kids, as

well. Deon who was 9 at the

time and Alyssa who was 6.

Immediately I fell in love with

them. When I decided to

propose to Tiva, I spoke to my

sons. They were all for it and

said they just wanted me to be

happy. I then approached Alyssa

Listed from bottom left; Cammeren, Alyssa, Tiva, Aliya, Collier, Me, and Deon.

and Deon to ask them what they thought, and Deon gave me the third

degree. In the end Alyssa, and Deon gave their blessing. I proposed within

a year of meeting Tiva.

I met with my doctors during an appointment when they gave me

horrible news. They told me that the cancer in my liver had progressed to

stage 4. Tiva was with me when I was told that, without the liver

transplant, I only had a short time left to live. When I got this news I got

depressed and decided that I couldn't marry Tiva. I didn't want to be a burden. I tried to break up with her and end the engagement. She sat me down one day and made me tell her what was going on. I told her that I didn't want to be a burden, and that's when she grabbed my hand and said, "I am not going anywhere; we are in this together!" At that point, I knew she was the one.

On July 10, 2007, we got married in Hawaii on The Big Island. It was like something out of a romantic movie. We had an early morning wedding. We had to leave the condo where we were staying at 4:30 am. It was still dark out as we literally drove up the side of a

mountain. I remember the two-lane road with no safety rail to keep you from driving off the side of the cliff which was a straight drop down. When we got there, we were separated. Tiva had her makeup done by a professional makeup artist. We got dressed in our own dressing rooms, and it was about an hour and a half before I saw her again. We met as we both came in from opposite sides of the Garden. I could not believe my eyes;

Tiva was beyond gorgeous.

We walked down to the beach as the sun began to rise above us and

took pictures and video. More pictures and video were taken as we walked

back to the place which was properly named Heaven's Gate. We were

married in the garden of the

property, which had waterfalls and

everything. Even though we were

elated to be marrying one another

and combining our families, my

illness was still this dark cloud

looming

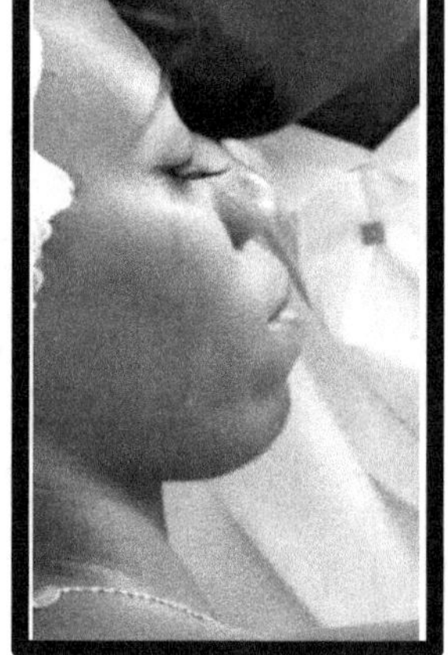

over our heads. Once we got back to Illinois and our

normal routines, I was informed that I was placed on

the transplant list. I was placed on the transplant list

in June of 2007 and asked if I would consent to

receiving a Hep C positive liver because they could

cure it after the transplant. I agreed to it.

CHAPTER FIFTEEN

THREE-AND-A-HALF MINUTES

I looked through the window of death and walked back

through the door of life.

It was a cold November Saturday morning at 3:45 am, when I got the long-awaited call. *"Can you be at the hospital within the hour? We have a liver for you,"* the male voice on the other line said, pleased to deliver the news. He paused for my answer.

I stammered, "Yes, of course!" Shock began to set in even before I hung up the phone. My initial excitement was soon followed by a sense of panic and dread. I had never had a major surgery of any kind before and didn't know what to expect. I began to make excuses, but my new wife quickly got up and started getting dressed.

She looked at me and simply said, "I am not losing you, get dressed!" I smiled nervously and pushed to snap myself out of it.

We got to the hospital, where we were met with family. I was surrounded, and that helped ease some of the nerves. The medical staff eventually came into the room and told me and my family that it was time. My wife walked by my gurney, and we shared nervous stares in complete silence. When we got to the double doors, they told her she couldn't go any further. I couldn't even begin to express my love to her. The only words I could utter were, "It will be okay; God is in control. I will see you when I wake up, and I love you."

She told me that she loved me too through her teary, bloodshot eyes, and off they took me. They got me on the cold steel table and prepared me for the surgery. When they were ready, they told me to count backward from ten. I began to count: *ten, nine, eight, seven...* The next thing I saw was blinding light all around me. It was brighter than the sun, but you could look into it because it didn't hurt your eyes. There was this overwhelming sense of peace and unconditional love that I can't even begin to describe. I made out two forms in the light. There was no verbal communication, but I was mentally told, "You will be okay; it is not your time, and you have to go back." The next thing I heard was this rhythmic noise of the breathing machine and my brother talking to me. I couldn't see anything because the room was pitch black. I began to struggle, but I was strapped down and had this tube down my throat. I struggled harder because it felt like I was breathing through a straw. I heard the doctors tell Tiva that if I didn't calm down, they would have to put me back under.

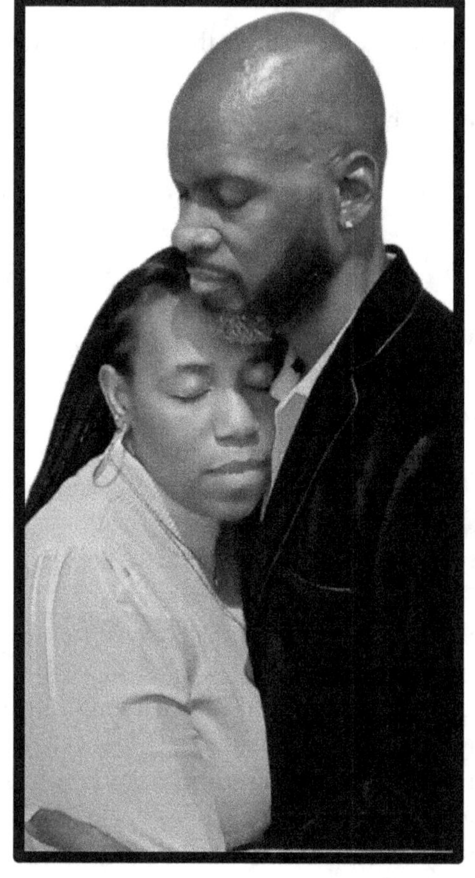

Tiva came over and began whispering in my ear, "I am here, babe, calm down."

About the longest hour later, I was off the breathing tube and in the ICU. The doctors told me not to speak because they had just pulled the breathing tube out. Tiva stood by my bedside with this strange look on her face. She stepped out of the room, and while she was gone, I overheard two nurses speaking about someone who had coded. I had a pen and paper the nurses gave me to communicate with Tiva, so I used that to ask questions. I was curious

because it sounded like they were talking about someone in the room next to me. They quickly tried to shut down the conversation by changing the subject when the doctor stood in the doorway of my room. He stood there staring with this odd look on his face. I kept writing questions, and that's when I found out from the doctor what happened. I thought it was the next day after the surgery, but I found out that I had been in a medically induced coma for a week. I was told that my new liver had an extra valve that my old liver did not have.

They sutured the valve and put me into recovery. While I was in recovery, I began bleeding out through that suture. A nurse found me and began life saving measures, but by the time the doctors got me back on the operating table, I had crashed. I was told that I was dead for three-and-a-half minutes. Shortly after I learned what happened, Tiva came back into the room. She had tears in her eyes, which I thought was about what I had just learned. I asked her if that was why she was crying, and she shook her head no. I asked why she was crying, and she just stared at me. I asked a couple more times, and she handed me a small bag with booties in it. After about a minute it hit me. "You are pregnant?" I wrote frantically. She smiled and slightly nodded yes with tears still streaming from her eyes.

My heart began racing, and the stats on my machines started going crazy. As the nurses and doctors began running into the room, I prematurely began trying to yell in excitement, "I am pregnant, I am pregnant!" In 2008 our baby girl was born. We decided to name her Aliya (which means "most high"), and we gave her the middle name Grace for the grace that God had bestowed on me to see me through the liver transplant. The recovery from that transplant was not an easy one. They reopened me two more times after the initial surgery. I remember being stressed out and pacing the floor in

a lot of pain at about two or three

in the morning. I was talking to

God with tears in my eyes when I

saw this flash of light from the

corner of my eye. I turned my

head, but I didn't see anything;

however, I felt this overwhelming

sense of peace wash over me. The

My daughter Aliya and I.

same overwhelming peace I had felt when I was in that light I spoke about

earlier. I did eventually recover. I was cancer free, hepatitis free, and I was

healthy again. I was able to get back in the gym. I advanced my career, and

life was once again great. I had a new liver and a new lease on life.

CHAPTER SIXTEEN

THE HARDEST DECISION

My brother Terrence was my best friend and like a father figure to me. We were both really sick. He needed a kidney at the same time that I nccdcd thc liver. We were both listed around the same time. My brother helped me during my recovery even though he was pretty sick. As I recovered, and began to

regain my health, he was beginning to diminish in his. The roles switched, and now I was helping to take care of him.

One morning I got a phone call, "Your brother fell in the bathroom, and he is bleeding and unconscious!" My sister n law asked me if they should get him into their car and drive him to the hospital or call an ambulance.

I said, "Call an ambulance!" I met my brother at the hospital and found him awake and talking.

We were always happy to see each other, and I walked in and asked, "What are you doing man? You forget how to use the bathroom or something?"

He chuckled and said, "Don't make me laugh; this morphine hasn't kicked in yet."

My brother and I continued talking, but he kept staring at the ceiling. In the middle of his sentence, he would look at the ceiling and then back at me.

Finally, I asked, "What are you looking at?"

He said, "You don't see that?"

I asked, "See what?"

He said, "You don't see Mom?"

I looked up and then back at my brother and said, "No, I don't see anything.

He looked back at the ceiling again and paused, then said, "Never mind," and continued on with our conversation.

I was not very happy with the care that the hospital was giving my brother, so I tried to do everything I could to get him transferred to the hospital where his primary care team was. This was also the same hospital that did my transplant. The fight was hard because of my brother's condition. They didn't want to take responsibility if something were to happen to him during the transport from one hospital to the other. Christmas Eve came, and while I was out doing some last-minute Christmas shopping, I got a call.

"Mr. Hanks," a frantic voice said, "this is Memorial Hospital. Your brother has gone into arrest, and we have been performing resuscitation. We are calling to find out if you would like for us to continue resuscitation procedures?"

I was so shocked. I quickly answered, "Yes! Save my brother!" I stopped everything I was doing and rushed to the hospital. I spoke to God all the way there, hoping and praying Terrence would be okay. When I got to his room, I was met by doctors who said that they got his heart going again, but that his brain was not showing any response. They put him under heavy sedation. They wanted a little time to see if his brain would start showing any signs of response. About two weeks later, we were called back to the hospital to discuss my brother's condition. It wasn't good. They said that he was

brain dead. They began to discuss taking my brother off life support. Once again, I was filled with anger and sadness. My oldest brother and sister left the decision up to me about taking Terrence off life support to try to give me closure. The doctor began dancing around my questions when I talked about the possibility of him coming back. Finally, I had enough of the dancing and snapped and cursed at the doctor, telling him, "Prove to me my brother is brain dead."

My sister, who is the oldest, called my name the same way my mother used to. "We weren't raised to act like that and treat people that way!" she quickly responded.

She was right, but this man was trying to convince me to give up hope. They took my brother off the sedation. As I looked into his eyes and called his name, I grabbed his hand. I looked for any sign of my brother, *any* response at all, but he wasn't there. I made the hardest decision in my life, to take him off life support the night of January 1, 2009. I chose to do it that night because his birthday was January 2, and I wanted him to pass on the same day he was born. We were asked a question that once again filled me with anger at first, but after thinking about it I agreed. They asked if we wanted to donate our brothers' organs. That question, at the time it was asked, felt like an ironic dagger in my chest. In hopes of helping someone else, I could not do anything but agree to it. They came back and said that he had MRSA, which is a staph infection. They said that it is usually resistant to antibiotics, so he was not a viable donor.

My oldest brother, my sister, and I met back at the hospital that night. We gave the go ahead and they shut down his life support. About fifteen minutes afterward, my sister and oldest brother began trying to get me to leave with them. I didn't want to leave my brother. They finally talked me into leaving with them, or so I made them believe. I walked to the parking lot with them and even got into my car and started it up, but I just stalled and waited for them to leave. My sister even drove up next to my car, telling me, "Go straight home, Phillip, there is nothing else you can do here."

I smiled and waved and said, "Okay." No sooner were they both out of the parking lot than I turned my car off and went right back upstairs. I sat with my brother, talking to him and praying over him. He began laboring and struggling to breathe, and I couldn't take the sounds of it anymore. I said my final goodbyes and kissed him on his forehead. I wasn't angry like I was with my mother. I think I was more defeated. My brother and I used to joke around about who was going to get their transplant first. We never thought about one of us not making it. I felt guilty; why me? Why couldn't they save him? Why did I get the transplant, and he didn't? I had received some kind of peace when the chaplain came to see us the day before in the hospital. The chaplain said that my brother, who did not go to church, asked her for prayer before he went into arrest.

Thank You

God, there are days that I take for granted all the blessings that you have given to me;
Days when I walk in blindness, like your love I don't see.

It's amazing that your are with me even when I give into sin;
Everyday you remind me not to give up, and to repent and try again.

If you want to hear God laugh tell him what your plans are in life;
Just when I said I was done with dating he introduced me to my wife.

When I thought the expiration date on my life was near I made my peace;
He laughed again and so no my son I will cure you and give you a new lease.

Not only that but I will give you an awesome story to tell;
Oh yeah and here is a little blessing for you and your wife as well.

We will Name her Aliya which means most high;
And the middle name Grace for the Grace that you had on my wife and I.

Thank you God for all the things that you have done for me and more;
But most of all for the things that you still have in store.

OUT OF NOWHERE

Good is never great, until worse happens.

2010 would turn out to have so many challenges and heart aches that pulled this close family even closer. Tiva's father, Ronald, had a series of strokes. The last stroke landed him in the hospital. They told him that he had to have brain surgery to relieve pressure. He refused to have the surgery done regardless of the fact that they said without the surgery, the next stroke could kill him. My mother-in-law called me and asked me to come to the hospital and talk to him. She said that he loved and respected me and that he might listen to me. My father-in-law stands at 6'6, with an athletic basketball build. He is dark complected with short black wavy hair and a goatee.

Tiva and I came to the hospital, and I asked to have a private moment with him. I asked my father-in-law to just hear me out. I told him how his family still needed him and what could happen if he didn't have the surgery. I told him that we still had to get out on the golf course together, and that he had so much more to do as a father. He dropped his head in thought. He looked up at me and reluctantly said, "Ok, I will do it." I was in shock and awe. I never had a father, but I felt a connection with my father-in-law. I never knew until that point that he felt the same about me. Unfortunately, he later suffered another stroke which left him with aphasia. Aphasia affects a person's ability to express and understand written and spoken language, so it is like he is trapped in his own body. He now has developed dementia, and although he still recognizes us, he often becomes confused and there are times he will call one of us by his siblings or mother's name.

Tiva has a little brother, my brother in law, Ron Jr. He was only 14 at the time that all of this was going on. Ron is about 6 foot tall and lanky like I was. He is dark complected and looks just like his father. He would always tell me how happy he was to have a big brother. Tiva's aunt Pat is considered the matriarch of the family. She reminds me of my godmother, with her rough exterior but inside she is filled with love. Auntie Pat is about 5'2 with a light complexion and short hair. She is very boisterous and is no nonsense. Tiva's other aunt Crystal is who they refer to as the "baby" of the family. She is light complected with long hair that she always keeps pinned up except on special occasions. Auntie Crystal has a huge heart and is the go-to aunt for information. They say if you don't want everyone to know, don't tell Auntie Crystal. Tiva's family dynamic is huge, and to be accepted into this family and respected is an honor.

Later that year, we found out that Tiva's mother, Beverly, developed stage 4 lung cancer. Beverly beat mouth cancer 22 years prior when Tiva was 14 years old. It truly hurt because of the relationship I had with her. She reminded me so much of my mother in the way that she was

a huge cheerleader. She was vibrant and full of energy. She stood about 5'4, with a very thin athletic build. She was light complected with long black hair that graced her shoulders. She had this animated but infectious laugh that made you laugh even

if you didn't know the reason you were laughing. Whenever I would do something that would impress Tiva or the family, she would just say, "I am not surprised, that's my Phillip." Beverly fought hard and was making a lot of progress until an issue outside of her control created significant stress for her.

Going into 2010, we celebrated her 60th birthday in December, she passed away that January. The circumstances were so similar to my mother passing and that it hit me hard. At her birthday party we sat together. She grabbed my hand and as she began to tear up, she made me make a

promise to her. She made me promise that I would take care of everyone which included her baby boy Ron Jr. I agreed and told her I would. Shortly after making that promise, I stepped away and broke down. I knew what was going on and what she meant, even though I still held out hope. I took that promise to heart and raised Ron as my own. We also abided by my mother-in-law's wishes and took over her house in Joliet that she had built from the ground up. We thought it was a good idea that Ron, who was 15 now, would go to the high school that my mother-in-law intended him to go to. He would also still have his friends and the familiar surroundings to ease the loss of his mother, and his father as much as possible.

Life was good as we fell into a routine and a normal life. You would never know we were a blended family until you began getting into the details. I began climbing the ladder in my IT career. From 2010 I was a server and network engineer. By 2012 I became a supervisor and by 2013 I became an IT manager. I applied myself to raising my family and advancing my career. By 2014 I was a Senior IT manager. I suffered a small setback in 2015. I got up like any other morning, got dressed for work, but I had major, excruciating pain in my abdomen. I pushed to go to work telling Tiva I was fine and continued to get dressed. Tiva left for work before me that day. We usually left at the same time but this day I was moving very slowly. God is with us always and promises to never leave us nor forsake us. He was definitely with me that day. By the time I was dressed the pain increased to a point that my objective changed from getting to work to getting to the hospital. I crawled down the stairs and barely managed to get to my car. I threw myself into my car and began driving myself to the hospital. I ran two stop lights and avoided one serious accident.

I got to the emergency area and threw my car into park. Security came out to tell me I couldn't park there, but with one look he quickly grabbed a wheelchair and wheeled me in. They took me straight to the back. They said I had a bowel obstruction that if I would have waited could have burst. They transferred me from the hospital in Joliet to the hospital on the south side of Chicago by ambulance. They took me straight in and performed emergency surgery. I recovered from that setback and kept striving in my career and by 2017 I became an IT Director. I was once asked when I first got into IT what my long-term goal was, and I said I wanted to become an IT Director or Chief Information Officer.

December of 2018, my family and I spent the holidays with our relatives in Texas. Tiva's cousin Rona, her husband Mark and their kids, Marcus, Mackenzie and Mia. Rona and her husband Mark Rona relocated to Texas for a job opportunity and a better life. Rona lost her mother earlier in 2018. Rona's mother was Tiva's auntie, Diane. This was another aunt that I admired and was really close with. She was average height, light complected with long black hair and she wore glasses. This aunt was known to be the life of the party, and was very loving. This aunt would call out of the blue just to check in on me and the family and we shared a lot of laughs. She worked downtown and on her way to work one morning tripped over some loose pavement and broke her leg. She had to have the leg operated on and did well. She was moved to a recovery center where

Listed fom left to right; Aliya, Me, Tiva, Alyssa, Deon, Ron, and Collier

she was not given her heart medication in a timely fashion. She passed due to a heart attack and it took everyone back by shock.

Tiva and I raced to the rehab facility in disbelief. When we arrived Tiva's cousin Kanika was there with her mother, auntie Pat. I fell into that step up role feeling like I had to do what to help. I got a facetime call from Rona where she asked me to go into the room to show her mother to her. I tried to console Rona and avoid what she was asking me to do. She wouldn't take no for an answer and because I knew that pain so well I fulfilled her request. Later that year we went to surround her with family from Chicago. It was such a great time and she was so happy that we came that we decided to do it again in 2019. It was kind of awesome to get out of the Chicago winter and stand next to Santa Claus on the front lawn with

a t-shirt and shorts on. My youngest son challenged me to a basketball game. I guess he wanted to see if the old man still had it. We got on the court, and in the middle of the  game, he went to make a layup. I simply waved my hand in his face, but when I did that, a pain shot up my arm and down my back.

I shrugged it off, thinking that maybe I pulled a muscle or something. The pain intensified throughout the

game, but I fought through it and finished. By the time we got back to my wife's cousin's house, I was begging for pain medication. They gave me 800 mg ibuprofen tablets. I started following the recommended dose, which was two tablets every 4 hours. The pain was still unbearable, so I switched to every 2 hours, then to every hour, down to every half an hour, until my wife and her family took the pain meds from me. I suffered for three days until we got back to Chicago. The next morning, my wife did something that helped save my life. She forced me to go to the hospital. The hospital kept me for a month and a half while they tried to figure out why I was in so much pain.

Tragedy struck again. The hospital couldn't figure out the source of

my pain, but upon discharging me

from the hospital, they gave me

bone-chilling news. They told me

that I needed a new liver, and my

kidneys were in 4th stage renal

failure. They also told me that I

would need to start dialysis

immediately, and I was given a

death sentence. They informed me

that they were not going to do the

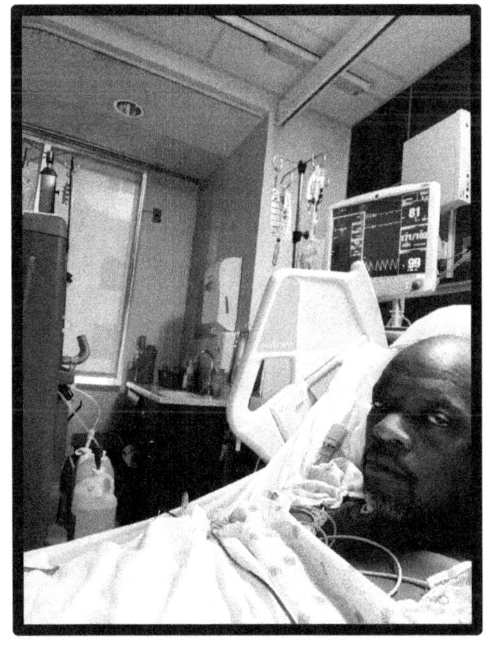

new transplant. I was devastated, shocked and angry. I began thinking

about how my death would impact my kids. My older kids were just

embarking on their lives, and I would not be there to help them navigate

through life. I wouldn't see my children get married or have kids. My

youngest daughter and I had this bond that would be broken, and where

would that leave her? My wife is a strong woman, but when I saw how her mother's death affected her, I wondered if my death would take her over the edge.

They were so matter of fact about it. Tiva's response was, "Babe, let it go, we don't want them to do the transplant anyway." She went on to say that if they could be so matter of fact about it then we didn't want them to do it anyway.

We went to the 4th largest hospital in the City of Chicago where they informed my wife and me about why the other hospital refused to do the surgery. They showed me on an X-ray where the pulmonary vein was blocked off with the scar tissue preventing proper blood flow to the major organs that the pulmonary vein fed. The hospital also informed me that they could not try to do a new transplant with the pulmonary vein in the condition that it was in. It would not only be extremely risky but very difficult. But the hospital didn't give up on me; they came up with a game plan.

They inserted a tube in my chest that went directly to my heart and started me on dialysis. Then they went into the pulmonary vein and tried to clean up as much of the scar tissue as they could and put in a stent to re-open the blockage. I was filled with hope when the surgeons came to get me and take me down for the procedure. I stayed in a positive mindset, telling myself, *When I wake up, they are going to tell me how successful they were and how everything is going to be fine.* The surgeons tried three times, and three times they failed. Three times I filled myself with hope and encouraged myself. After the third try, the main surgeon came into my hospital room with tears in his eyes, and the nurses that came in with him were solemn. He choked up when he said, "I am sorry, we have done everything we can for you. There is nothing else that we can do."

I asked, "Are there any other options?"

The surgeon said, "One minute," and stepped out of my room.

While he was speaking to one of his nurses in the hallway, my wife turned to me with tears in her eyes and said, "You better not give up; I am not ready to lose you!"

The surgeon stepped back into the room and told us about a

surgeon in an Indianapolis hospital called Indiana University (IU) Health

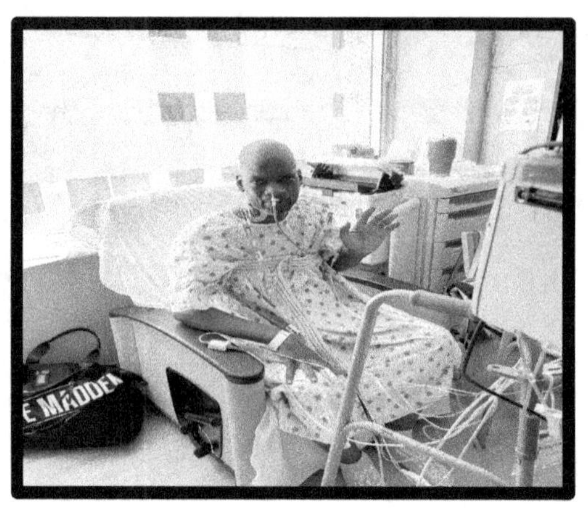

by the name of Doctor Mangus. Doctor Mangus specialized in hard cases like mine. I set up a consultation with him and his team. My wife and I drove the three-and-a-half hours to Indianapolis for a consultation.

He told me how difficult my case was and hesitated. You could tell he was

about to say that he wouldn't take it. He said that, because of the scar

tissue, if he was going to give me the transplant, he would cut the

pulmonary vein above the scar tissue and remove it along with the organs

attached. He went on to say that he would then remove the donor's organs

with the piece of vein that had the scarring in mine and attach it to me.

The doctor continued on to say, "The chances of this working are

50/50, and to give you full disclosure,

this is an extremely difficult case. I'm

not sure it will even work!"

Not only did I have all of this

scar tissue, but stomach transplants are

extremely rare. He said that he had a

patient that just passed the previous

week. The patient had a stomach and

liver transplanted and did great. She

went home, but within less than a month

she became septic and died. I put my

Dr. Magnus, my surgeon.

best poker face on, before asking to be excused to use the restroom. I

couldn't show my true reaction because I didn't want to freak my wife out.

I went into the bathroom and my whole demeanor broke. I am not a

germaphobe, but I like cleanliness. All of that went out of the window as I

fell to my hands and knees in tears on the public bathroom floor.

I called out to God in a hushed, but panicked, voice. I said, "God, so this is it? This is how I die?" I went on to call on Jesus saying, "Jesus, help me! I don't know what to do! You said to ask *anything* in your name and you would do it. Well, I am asking you to HELP ME!"

I heard, *I have not left you in all of this time, why would I leave you now?* The events surrounding my 2007 transplant immediately came to mind. I got up off the floor and made my way to the sink. I looked at myself in the mirror and saw that I was a mess. My eyes were bloodshot from crying, and I still had tears all over my face. I had to clean myself up because I didn't want my wife to see me like this. I cleaned myself up and regained my composure. As I grabbed the bathroom door to leave and return to the consultation, I heard, *I am going to use you as a testament to MY glory!* I felt that same peace and calm wash over me that I felt when I was surrounded by that light in 2007. I rejoined the

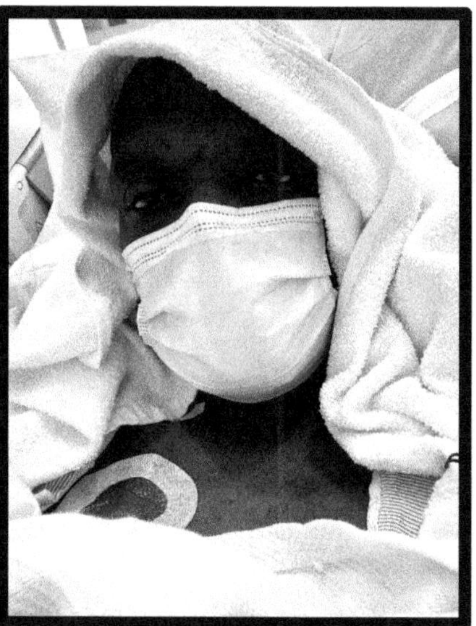

consultation, and the doctor said he would take my case and asked me what I wanted to do.

I looked at my wife and asked, "So what do you think?"

She looked at me like I had two heads and said, "What choice do we have?"

I looked back at the doctor and said, "Okay, let's do it!"

I was listed December 31, 2020, in the middle of the Covid epidemic. I asked what would happen if I got Covid, and I was told, "Don't get Covid." It was truly scary. April rolled around and my 50th birthday was coming up. My birthday is April 23, and this birthday was monumental for me because I never thought I would live to see it. Three days before my birthday, I received a call.

"Hello, Mr. Hanks, we have a donor for you, how soon can you get here?"

The hospital in Indianapolis was three-and-a-half hours away. I remember joking with the doctor and his team saying, "Oh, this gives me a reason to speed!"

They said, "Well, actually we will give you a letter. If you get pulled over, show this letter and they will let you go. They may even give you an escort."

Normally I would have been excited, because I have a heavy foot anyway. But when I got this call, I started moving in slow motion. I was scared. My wife began calling people to inform them that I got the call. Family and friends began calling and wanted to pray. It reminded me of what I was told in the bathroom, *"I am with you,"* and *"I am going to use you as a testament to my glory."* Remembering that calmed me enough to get out of the door and onto the expressway. But for some reason I could not calm completely down and shake this bad feeling. I was so grateful for everyone that was praying for me. My wife has a much larger family than mine, filled with aunts and cousins that my wife grew up with. Two of my wife's cousins are like sisters to her. As a matter of fact, when I decided to propose to Tiva, it was at her cousin Rona's wedding. When the wedding was over, I presented the ring to Tiva's mother and father and asked her parents for Tiva's hand in marriage.

Her mother was elated, and her father said, "you seem to make my daughter happy, and if she is happy then I am ok with you."

Tiva's mother called her from the main chapel where she was taking pictures with Rona and the wedding party, to the back where everyone had gathered waiting for the bride and groom. Her mother wrangled her over to me and said, "ok go!" I nervously dropped to one knee and pulled out the ring in one fluid motion. I said, "I know we have been dating for a little while now, and I told you that I wasn't playing with you…. Will you marry me?"

Tiva jumped back as she gasped and covered her mouth. I could barely make out what everyone was saying because all I could focus on was Tiva, and not the commotion going on around me. It felt like I was down on my knee for at least 20 mins with my heart in my throat before I heard Tiva's mother yell, "answer him, Tiva!"

She finally answered… "yes."

I got up relieved and we hugged and kissed for hours afterwards. I prayed to God that night and consistently afterward to bless me to make it through the illness of fourth stage liver cancer. Tiva's family surrounded me with so much love and support. Tiva's second cousin who is like a sister to her is Kanika. Her and her husband Jermaine opened their home to Tiva and our family. They stayed about 20 mins away from where my hospital and doctors were. They have two beautiful daughters Kennedy who is now 14 and Kensington who is 7. Jermaine and I became very close. I look at him as a brother. In my darkest hour he kept me filled with encouragement. He is an old soul with so much wisdom and clarity. He prayed with me and helped me get rid of the jitters and, once again, reminded me that God had me. He called his cousin, who is a pastor, and we prayed together with Tiva. It was a mountain moving prayer! My wife's cousin Rona, the cousin we visited in Texas, called during that drive. She conferenced in her father, who is a pastor, and we also prayed together.

I had a conversation with each of my children. I gave instructions on what I expected from each child if anything were to happen to me during the surgery. They in turn reminded me of how they were raised and fed my words of encouragement back to me. We got to the hospital, and it was crazy. Due to Covid, my wife could not go upstairs with me. Once again, I was unnerved. They got me prepared for surgery and put me in my room. As I sat there in nothing but a hospital gown, I stayed on the phone with my wife. We got there at midnight, but it wasn't until 10:00 am that morning that we found out the transplant was a no go. Dr Mangus said that the pancreas was defective and because all of the organs had to come from the same donor, he decided to cancel the surgery. After staying up all night, I looked at it and said that it could have gone horribly wrong. They could have transplanted the organs and then found out that the pancreas was defective.

As we drove back home and I was going over my thoughts and what just happened. My wife was frantically typing away on her phone. We got home and I crashed. The next day was April 22, and I was kind of relieved that I wouldn't be spending my birthday in the hospital. The day of my birthday was kind of quiet. I had a number of birthday wishes, but my wife was acting very strange.

Later that afternoon she came in and said, "It is time to get dressed."

She had taken me with her earlier that day to treat me to some new clothes. The outfits she helped me put together were like something you would wear to a black-tie event. We got dressed and she put the address to where we were going in my GPS. I pulled up, and it looked like a storefront from the outside. Before I could ask any questions, my wife and daughter jumped out of the car and told me to come with them. We walked up to this storefront, and before I could open the door for my wife and daughter, it burst open, and a photographer and videographer came out. They began snapping pictures and taking videos. I walked into the venue, and everyone was there! "Surprise!" they screamed. It turned out that when Tiva was feverishly typing away on her phone, she was telling everyone that my surprise birthday party was back on.

The party was epic. My 50th birthday was like no birthday I'd ever had, and two days later I got the ultimate birthday gift. I received another phone call the night of April 26, 2021.

"Hello, Phillip, we have another donor for you. We need you to come back to the hospital, how soon can you get here?"

I replied, "About three-and-a-half hours." This time around, I felt more at ease, and I wasn't as nervous.

My wife was allowed to come in with me this time, because Covid restrictions had slightly lifted. They prepared me for the surgery and my wife, and I began the wait. We laughed, joked, and reminisced to pass the time, and before we both knew it, they came to get me. My wife walked by my bedside as they wheeled me down to the operating room. We arrived at the double doors again just like last time, only this time my wife, who had been so calm and collected, was at her wits' end. Her eyes were swollen and red. I asked the transporters for a minute to speak to her. I tried to calm her and told her that God was with me, and I was going to be okay. She shook her head in agreement, but I still felt like she was very upset. I asked her for her cellphone and called her Aunt Pat, who is the matriarch of her family and one of my biggest supporters. I also called both of her cousins, Rona and Kanika, as well as three of her best friends.

I asked them all to be with her and make sure that she was okay. I said that she really needed them right now, and if anything were to happen during the surgery, and I didn't make it, to please form a wall of love around her and the kids. I kissed my wife again and told her that I would see her when I woke up. They wheeled me in and got me on the table. "Are you ready?" they asked. They placed the mask on my face and told me to take deep breaths and count backward from ten. I began counting, *ten, nine, eight, seven...* When I woke up, I was on a breathing tube, which I was told to expect. I asked for pen and paper and began

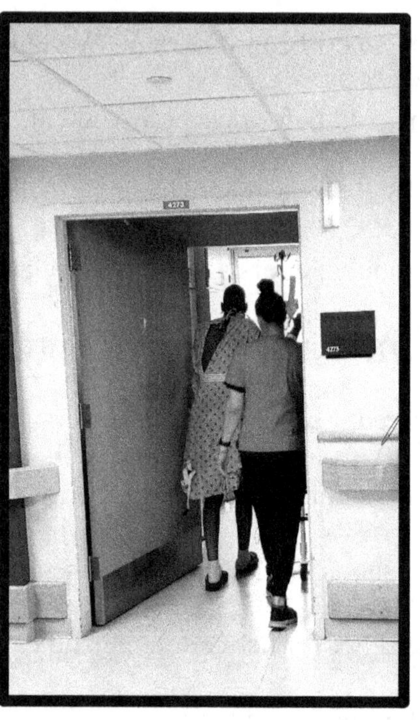

writing notes. I was still groggy when I wrote my very first note, which was "I love you, Tiva." As I became more alert, it got harder and harder to stay in rhythm with the breathing machine and let it breathe for me. I wrote another note to Tiva, asking her to ask them to take me off the machine. They denied my request, saying it was too soon to remove the tube.

It was a two-day surgery. The first day, I received a pancreas, liver, upper and lower intestines, and stomach. I didn't even know that you could transplant a stomach. The first surgery took eight hours. They said that if they took the tube out, they would have to put it back in for surgery the next day. I still insisted and kept insisting. Even though it was out of the norm, they finally relented and removed the tube. They were shocked

Breathing tube is still in so he asked for paper and pencil for this….

at how well I was doing. I wanted to get up and out of the bed, but they would not allow that. They came the next day and took me back down to surgery to transplant the kidney. When I woke up this time, there was no breathing tube, just pain. It wasn't intense, but they gave me a morphine pump with a time-release button. The doctors and nurses told me to hit that button whenever I was in pain. They didn't want the pain to hinder my recovery. The more pain you are in, the less likely you will move around, and moving around is good to help with recovering.

I took the pain for as long as I could before hitting the button. The relief was instantaneous, but I have always heard about people getting addicted to pain medications, and I did not want to be a statistic. Within a day and a half of waking up from the second surgery, I remembered from the first liver transplant how important it was to get up and walk. I told Tiva that I wanted to get up. She wanted me to take it easy and not push myself so soon. I had this drive pushing me to get up, so I told my nurses and the doctors that I wanted to. Just like my wife, everyone wanted me not to push it. They sat me up and told me they were worried about me being dizzy and weak. When they sat me up, I felt fine outside of the pain. I got the first look at myself, and I had tubes and wires everywhere. I had the port that they put in my chest for dialysis, I had a tube in my neck, a feeding tube, a drainage tube, and so many more.

I protested and insisted, and finally the doctor told my nurse to call my physical therapist. The physical therapist came into the room and said, "If he wants to get up and walk, then let him get up and walk."

There was a team of people that surrounded my bed, moving tubes and wires and helping me get to the side of the bed. I dangled my feet off the side of the bed as they constantly asked me, "Are you okay? Do you feel dizzy? Do you want to lie back down?"

I said, "I am okay," as I pushed the pain button. I pushed myself forward and grabbed the walker they had waiting for me. I was on my feet. I took my first step, then second, and before I knew it, I was at the chair that was on the other side of the room. I sat down in that chair, as the reality of what had just happened slowly began to set in.

I couldn't believe it. I remember thinking, "Okay, so now I have to recover and get better. They said I had a fifty-fifty chance, and I am going to take it! Thank you, God!"

Each day, I pushed to walk further and further. I was supposed to be in the ICU for about a month, but I was only there for two weeks. When they came to move me out of the ICU, they tried to put me in a wheelchair and wheel me over to my room. I refused the wheelchair and walked. I was supposed to be in the hospital for about six months, but I was only in the hospital for two-and-a-half months. At the beginning of August, a trip to

Aruba that my wife and I were supposed to take, came up. Originally, we were not going to go because I was on the list and couldn't leave the country, and they could call at any time. I wanted to take my wife because she handled everything while I was down during the beginning of Covid, which we all know was a very stressful and scary time. When I began to doubt, she was right there to remind me that not only was she there, but that God was in control. She took care of me during my recovery and still continued to be a mother, staying on top of everything from the household to the kids.

She is an awesome first grade teacher. For example, during Covid, to handle remote learning, she created a virtual classroom with an avatar for each kid and herself in an interactive classroom that she used to keep the kids engaged and active. The virtual classroom made everyone from

her administration to her peers take notice. She has always been too

humble and modest to take credit for being the awesome teacher, mother,

and wife that she is, which is why I wasn't going to let this opportunity to

take her to Aruba pass by. It was a trip that all of Tiva's cousins were

going on to celebrate her cousin Rona's birthday. I petitioned my doctors

to let me take her on this trip, and they began going over how long I had

been in recovery and saying it was too soon. I would not relent and kept

asking.

Eventually, I decided that I was taking her. She deserved to go. She

had been very stressed trying to avoid Covid by every means. If I got

Covid they would not transplant me. She made sure every speck of the

house was sanitized. She followed every precaution, even when it came to

getting groceries. I moved forward and just purchased everything instead

of waiting on the doctor's approval. The next time the doctors and I spoke,

I asked again but told the doctor and his team that I had already paid for

the trip. The doctor and his team gave me their consent to go, with a

warning about Covid. They also wanted me to make sure I took precautions against overdoing it, as well as keeping the port that I still had

in my chest clean and dry. All of the other tubes had been removed. The

only tube I had left was the tube they originally put in my chest.

I was excited that I could take her but bummed out that I wouldn't

be able to do one of my favorite things, which is jet skiing. I lived for two

years with the fact that if the port got infected, it could kill me because that

tube was the one that went directly into

my heart. When I told my wife that we

were going, she was beside herself with

excitement. She had been cooped up for

so long due to Covid and my health. We

went and it was amazing. I felt great,

and we did a little bit of everything. We

went on an excursion that took us to the

top of a cliff in an off-road vehicle. It was a beautiful view overlooking the

sea and the mountainous scenery all around us. My wife and I walked over

to the cliff edge where there was an observatory. There was a hot spring

that was created by a volcano at the base of it. Tiva wanted to climb down the side of this cliff that was a little over a mile down, to get to this spring pool. For me, it looked too overwhelming to hike down, not to mention the climb back up. I told her I would stay at the top, inside the observatory, and watch from up there.

In a somber voice, she said, "Well, if you don't want to go then I will just sit here with you, and we can watch everyone else." I looked at the disappointment in her eyes as we began to watch everyone else go down the mountainside. I grabbed my wife by the hand and said, "Come on." We began climbing down the mountainside, and before we knew it, we reached the bottom. With a short walk from there, we made it to the hot spring. Tiva was like a kid and couldn't wait to get in. I hung out at the edge after helping her in because I could not get the port in my chest wet. After my wife and her cousins had their fun, it was time to go back. I was nervous about hiking back up the mountainside because everyone knows that it is easier going down then going back up. We started climbing and before we knew it, we were halfway back to the top. Tiva wanted to take a break because she was tired, but I wanted to keep going. We took a short break before finishing the climb. During the trip, everyone was worried about me and asking me how I was doing, but I felt great! We made it

back home without incident, and it was a remarkable trip. Can you believe

that just four months after a five-organ transplant, I hiked down the side of

a mountainside *and*

back up it?

CHAPTER EIGHTEEN

UPDATES ON LOVE, MEDICINE, & MIRACLES

The recovery on-going has been remarkable, and without any
issues. April 26, 2021, three days after my 50th birthday, I received a new liver, kidney, pancreas, upper and lower intestines, and a stomach. April 26, 2022, just three days after my 51st birthday, I celebrated my one-year

Me and Illinois Secretary, Jesse White

anniversary of that transplant with Secretary of the State of Illinois Jesse

White. He caught a story about my transplant that made the front page of the Chicago Tribune news paper. His team invited me down to his office and asked me to do a PSA about organ and tissue donation. After doing the PSA I was asked if I wanted to meet the Secretary. Meeting the Secretary was like speaking to an old family member. His heart out ways his stature. Jesse White became like an uncle or grandfather to me. In December of 2021 I became a

 new grandfather of a beautiful baby girl. I got to see my 13-year-old daughter walk across the stage and graduate 8th grade in May of 2022. I was able to attend my 22-year-old daughter's graduation from college in June of 2022. July 10 of 2022, my beautiful wife and I celebrated our 15th wedding

anniversary. I became a spokesperson for the organ and tissue donation program in Illinois and have had a commercial that ran all throughout the state.

Denishia (Denny), is now a grown woman with a beautiful daughter named Jordan. They not only saw the commercial but attended a kidney fair that I participated in on behalf of the Secretary of State. I was fortunate enough to make amends with her and give her the heartfelt apology that she deserved. We were always friends before, and it is nice to have that friendship back. I am a hopeful advocate for her as I found out that unfortunately she needs a kidney transplant. She has a living donor; however, she has developed antibodies in her blood. She is highly sensitized, which makes it hard to get a match for a transplant. I continue to encourage her and others to advocate for themselves and keep pushing and pressing with hope in mind.

Although a lot of my circumstances have not always been ideal, I have always had one constant — God! We are all naturally wired to blame something or someone else for our circumstances when things go wrong. I have learned that changing takes considerable effort. There is a lot of discomfort, uncertainty, and hard work on a daily basis.

It takes time to develop and grow, and you are never too old to grow and learn. I am still trying to grow and learn daily. I am also trying to mend fences and clean up disasters where I can.

CHAPTER NINETEEN

A WORD OF ENCOURAGEMENT

When you come to a fork in the road, a choice between

hope and despair, choose to walk the road less

traveled—the road of hope.

People have thought differently from each other for decades, and many people have different outlooks on life, but it is clear that your mindset can impact your outcomes. Johns Hopkins Medicine has shown through research that a positive and hopeful mindset allows people to navigate stress and challenges better. A positive mindset can also lead to higher levels of wellbeing, and measurably affect physical healing. Find a way forward and don't fall into a pattern of getting stuck in a negative mindset where you let negativity keep you down.

Ask yourself constructive questions. *How can I make the most of the situation? What are my options? What kind of research can I do to help me with the situation? Who can I ask to get more information?* When you engage in a negative mindset, you are engaging in a mindset that does not offer any solutions and can cause depression and other non-productive questions. Questions like *Why me?* or *What's the use in trying?* Life can be stressful sometimes, but sometimes the biggest source of stress is your own mind and negative thinking.

Keep in mind that you should always test your expectations, but that adopting a positive set of assumptions can help you reach different conclusions you might not otherwise explore. What we believe and assume, we hold to be true. Our beliefs come from real-life experiences. Our values and beliefs affect the quality of our life, our work, and our relationships. Since what we believe is what we have experienced, what we tend to think becomes founded on our reality. I believe that since I was a child, God has been with me. I think about what I heard in the bathroom when I thought my life was coming to an end. *"I am going to use you as a testament to my glory." Inside Edition* covered my story, along with many other media outlets and reporters. I did not seek them out, they sought me.

I think a lot about my mother and my brother, and how I miss them tremendously. There are times when I feel lonely, but I remember God's words: *I have been with you all of this time, why would I leave you now?* A lot of people have asked me about my mindset. I

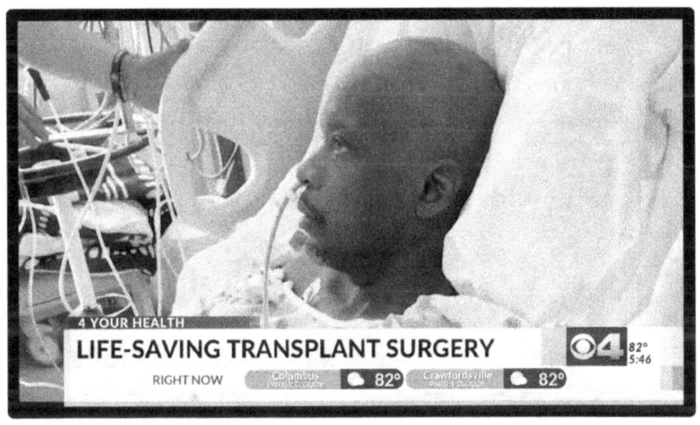

believe that every day we are faced with questions, and how we answer those questions affects every decision we make. We make choices with our words and our actions. Even if we choose to do nothing at all, that is still a choice and an action. It's common and easy to think negatively, but what we don't realize is we can do a lot of damage by doing that. When we think negatively, negative actions follow. If we think we cannot, then we can't! I believe what my mother always taught me: *"Through God anything is possible"* (Matthew 19:26).

I have come up with my own saying, "When the spirit of God enters the imagination, he brings a vision. Once we have the vision, the spirit of God brings belief. Once we have belief in God and the vision he has given us, our dreams can be brought to reality!" Through the spirit of God, the impossible becomes possible. Figuring out a way to do something, once we intend to do it, is achievable with faith in God. We need to learn how to look at life with our spiritual mindset and get beyond the negativity that surrounds us. If we learn to get in line with God's Holy Spirit, we can use his positive spirit to accomplish the impossible.

I only hope my experience is a witness and a testimony to the glory of God. I hope it enlightens and helps you to find the spirit of God, that he has hidden within every one of us. I hope my experience provokes deeper thoughts of positivity and inspiration! God has brought me through a lot of things and has done so much for me. God wants to do things for you, and through you too!

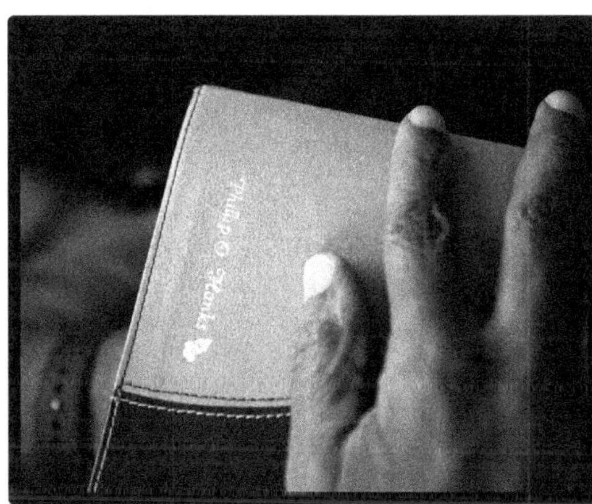

Jesus said, "You can ask for anything in my name, and I will do it." (John 14:14).

MORE MEMORIES

Listed from left; Me, Idelle, and Gerald.

Ex-NFL Coach of the Chicago Bears, Lovie Smith and Cammeren.

My grandmother and I.

Listed from left; Me, Eric and Gavin.

Listed from left; Me, AJ, Eric, and Gavin.

My grand-daughter, GiGi and I.

LifeGoesOn
Be an organ/tissue donor
Phillip Hanks needed five organ transplants to live. A decision by a complete stranger changed his story and saved his life.
Change someone's story.
Register at LifeGoesOn.com.
Five and Alive
Phillip and his wife, Tiva
JESSE WHITE
SECRETARY OF STATE

From left; Deon, Brittany (my new daughter-in-law), Tiva and I.

ABOUT THE AUTHOR

Phillip has witnessed the many facets of God's power in his 51 years. He's experienced adversity from a rough childhood. He passed away during a 2007 liver transplant. He recovered, and in 2020, he was told he needed a new 5-organ transplant. In April of 2021 he received that transplant, which included a new liver, stomach, pancreas, upper and lower intestines, and kidney. He delivers a message of hope, faith, and

292

perseverance based on his own experiences and miraculous recoveries. He is currently a husband, a father of six, a grandfather of one little girl and another grandchild on the way. He currently lives in Illinois where he is an advocate for organ and tissue donation.